FAST & EASY VEGAN COOKBOOK

Fast & Easy VEGAN

COOKBOOK

100 Mouthwatering Recipes for Time-Crunched Vegans

JL FIELDS

photography by Marija Vidal

ROCKRIDGE
PRESS

To the compassionate animal activists whom I'm honored to call my dearest friends: Ethan Ciment, Michael Suchman, Laurie Clauss, Doug Schrepel, Cody Rilo, and Tyler Schiedel. I love each and every one of you, and I love the myriad ways in which you all advocate for justice for animals.

Contents

Introduction

Y ou likely picked up this book because the idea of fast and easy vegan cooking is appealing. Well, you're in good company, because I feel the same, and it's exactly how I cook. Now, that might surprise you. Shouldn't a six-time cookbook author and a culinary instructor be really into fancy cooking? Nope.

I have a feeling I might be a lot like you.

Over seventeen years ago, I became a vegetarian after a trip to Africa and an experience with a goat. As a gal from the Midwest, I certainly understood where meat came from, but there was something about witnessing a goat being slaughtered, stewed, and served. That was it for me. However, probably like many of you, I took a while to move from vegetarian to vegan. Truthfully, it wasn't nearly as dramatic. I was simply working with a nutritionist to "clean up" my diet and discovered after a couple of weeks that I hadn't consumed any animal products. "Hey," I thought, "this is easy!" So I went vegan. Of course, I realized it wasn't exactly simple because I had to relearn a lot—including cooking—because while I had been traipsing around the world for work, my husband was the primary cook in our home. After my plant-based conversion, he declared, "You're on your own!"

So there I was, a new vegan returning to the kitchen. I knew that the name of the game was going to be, *Get in, get out, and eat well.*

And that's what this book is all about. It's the way I've been cooking for years. You *can* do this easily, quickly, healthfully, and deliciously. I'm going to help you. I know that some of you aren't vegan, but you are motivated to eat more plant-based meals or you're trying to get your family to eat more plants. This book is for you, too. I've created recipes that are both familiar and will stretch your culinary muscles.

Typically, the biggest challenge for a new vegan is how to replace that piece of meat on the plate (also known as, "Where do you get your protein?"). In 2013, I coauthored *Vegan for Her* with Virginia Messina, one of the brightest vegan registered dieticians I know, and she broke it down so well. Focus on these five food groups—aptly named "The Fab Five"—vegetables, fruit, beans and legumes, nuts and seeds, and grains. That's it! After that, it's all about learning how to cook and prepare those food groups so that you get a wide variety of flavor, texture, and nutrition.

With the five food groups in hand, I began to batch cook—also known as meal prepping—on the weekend so that I would have what I needed during the week. In that process, I discovered that pressure cooking was an even quicker way to get meal prep done. I have an entire chapter in this book devoted to pressure cooking using either a stovetop pressure cooker or the Instant Pot®.

But we don't all meal prep, and those of us who do, don't do it every week. So, finding fast ways to get balanced meals on the table became my focus for cooking classes and the work I do with private clients. I love showing folks how a can of beans, a can of tomatoes, some chopped veggies, and a few spices can result in a thick, hearty, and flavorful pot of chili or stew in a matter of minutes. That's what you can expect to find in this book. I'm going to walk you through a variety of methods and techniques to meet your nutrition and flavor goals without spending a lifetime in the kitchen. And that's why this book is ideal both for people who are new to vegan cooking and long-time vegans who simply want to learn new ways to prepare vegan meals as quickly as possible.

Don't think of this book as the one to use to wow 12 dinner guests on a Saturday night.

Do think of it as the one just right for your real life.

We're not going to be using a lot of ingredients here. Cooking times and techniques will be short and direct. You'll learn how some appliances can provide shortcuts to meals, and you'll see I even have a chapter devoted to not cooking at all. Think of this book as the one you pick up on a Wednesday night after a long day of work. Turn to any page and there's a good chance you'll be eating happily and healthfully in about 30 minutes.

Okay, let's get into the kitchen and whip something up, fast and easy!

Black Bean and
Sweet Potato
Tacos, page 54

1

Vegan Meals Made Fast & Easy

Nine years ago, as a new vegan, I had many questions. What am I supposed to eat? Why eat *that?* How do I make . . . ? You get the idea. So I'm going to answer many of the common questions right here, before we start cooking. I want to demystify vegan cooking in general and get you excited about the culinary delights of plant-based cooking.

MORE THAN SALADS AND OREOS

Veganism—and the perception of it—has changed dramatically over the years. The old stereotypical image of hippies nibbling on twigs is a thing of the past. The new stereotype suggests that vegans just eat "junk food." However, if you're like me, you know that vegans are more complex than these stereotypes! First, there's nothing wrong with a wholesome bowl of leafy greens. Second, why not enjoy some of the awesome, new prepared vegan items available at the store? Just because it's store-bought, doesn't make it junk food.

New vegans and veg-curious folks do struggle to find a balance and might default to all salads or all chips. The good news is that salads are fantastic, especially when you treat them as a meal: Simply fill a bowl with your favorite raw vegetables and add cooked beans or quinoa and a creamy nut- or seed-based dressing. As for the so-called junk food, I say, go ahead and enjoy some vegan chips and snacks now and then. You could also slice up a couple of potatoes, bake or air-fry them, and just like that, you're eating a vegetable chip made at home!

Here are some of the common questions I'm asked:

What do vegans eat? It's not just kale and pasta, people! Remember the Fab Five (vegetables, fruit, beans and legumes, nuts and seeds, and grains)? That's a whole lot of variety, and all of these foods are available at grocery stores, well-stocked convenience markets, and even those big discount membership stores. Tofu, tempeh, and peanuts fall into the legume category, as do chickpeas and lentils.

Grains include quinoa, farro, barley, brown rice, millet, seitan (it's made from wheat gluten), and, yes, even pasta. See? Variety!

What's vegan? Don't roll your eyes! If you're vegan, you know there was a time when you wondered the same thing. All of the aforementioned foods are vegan because they contain no animal products. So let's rephrase: What's *not* vegan? Meat, poultry, pork, seafood, shellfish, eggs, dairy products, honey, and other bee products. You won't find any of those ingredients in this book.

Whoa. Will I be eating more to make up for not eating animal protein? Maybe. But maybe not. When you fill your plate with plants, you may notice that it takes fewer calories to sate your hunger because fiber, which veggies have a lot of, is filling; meat doesn't have any fiber.

Some people follow a plant-based diet to lose weight, and there's a good chance you can eat more and still lose weight because whole, plant-based foods are nutrient dense without being calorie dense. Like any way of eating, a vegan diet can support your health goals; it all depends on what you put on your plate.

EASY TO MAKE; FAST ON THE TABLE

I'd say the number one assumption is that vegan cooking is a complex and arduous process. Good news: it doesn't have to be. Listen, I cook for a living, and even I don't want to spend too much time in the kitchen or too much money on ingredients. I love cooking and I love eating, but I don't need to spend an entire day on either. And that's likely why you picked up this book—you want meals that are accessible and speedy. In most of these recipes, you'll get both. But in some, you'll get one or the other. This is by design. Overall, I want you to get in and out of the kitchen with minimal effort and a full and happy belly. But there are those occasions when you want the simpl-*er* version of a complex recipe, and I'm going to give you that, too.

This book offers a user-friendly layout:

No Cooking Required includes some raw recipes but mostly focuses on food that's ready to enjoy without cooking.

Thirty-Minute Meals are ideal for weeknight cooking after a long day or even for preparing in the morning before walking out the door.

Five Ingredients is a dream come true, and we'll only use five ingredients, excluding water, oil, vegetable broth, and salt and pepper, of course.

One-Pot Wonders focuses on streamlined stovetop creations, whether in a skillet, Dutch oven, or saucepan.

Bake It Right is all about the ease of sheet pan and casserole cooking.

No-Pressure Pressure Cooking recipes will get traditionally longer-cooking plant-based recipes on the table fast.

Kitchen Staples features DIY pantry staples that you'll want to keep on hand.

THE BALANCED MEAL

At the risk of sounding repetitive, the Fab Five are your building blocks and they're what I teach in my cooking classes. To create a balanced meal, you'll want to think about what you're eating throughout the day to make sure you get all five into your meals and snacks. A great place to start when planning lunch and dinner (and, for me, even breakfast) is with beans, greens, and grains. Right there you'll get three of your vegan food groups. Add a cashew sauce to a cooked dish, or chopped pecans or walnuts to a raw salad bowl and you've got four. Add fruit to granola or oatmeal in the morning, and you're getting grains and fruit; splash in some soy milk and you've got your beans.

See? Isn't this fun (*and easy*)?

Some of you may be focused on macronutrients, and you'll find that information for each recipe. Others simply want to eat healthfully, and you'll do just that because I've created recipes that are cholesterol-free, high in fiber, and only use healthy plant-based fats.

You also don't need to worry about the outdated notion of combining proteins. There was a time when healthcare professionals suggested that vegans and vegetarians had to eat foods in combination so they got all nine essential amino acids in one meal ("essential" means something the body can't produce on its own). Any food that contains all nine was called a "complete protein." This theory was debunked many years ago, and the position of the Academy of Nutrition and Dietetics is that "protein from a variety of plant foods eaten during the course of a day supplies enough of all essential amino acids when caloric requirements are met."

Bottom line: Eat the Fab Five and you're going to get all the nutrients you need. Deliciously.

Proteins Are Your Power Source

Let's address the elephant (they're vegan!) in the room. Where do we get our protein? If you've been vegan for a while, I'm guessing you just rolled your eyes. If you're new to this whole thing, you're thinking, "Finally! Help me!" As a long-time vegan I never, ever roll my eyes at the question, because before I was vegan, I had the same question.

Having taught thousands of people in cooking classes, I now know that's not the real question. The question is, "What do I put on my plate to replace the protein found in meat or dairy?"

Protein is found in all plant foods, and legumes are a good source of it. Legumes come in so many tasty varieties, including lentils (available in a rainbow of colors including black, green, brown, yellow, and red), chickpeas, black-eyed peas, kidney beans, and peanuts. (Did you know peanuts are a legume and not a nut?) Soybeans, in all their forms, are a particularly good source of protein. Try edamame, tempeh, and tofu, which range from 15 to 18 grams of protein per serving.

Confession time: I had to learn to love legumes. I grew up in the Midwest, where the only beans I was exposed to were canned pork and beans, green beans, and kidney beans in meat-heavy chili. I soon discovered that legumes are versatile, perfect in soup, enjoyed as tofu or tempeh, puréed into hummus or bean dip, simmered in a dal, and more.

Grains are also an important and tasty source of protein. Quinoa (technically a seed), rice in its many colorful varieties, farro, oats, corn, and many more—all are enjoyable as a simple side or part of a larger dish.

Another high-protein food is seitan, which delivers 20 grams of protein per serving. Also known as "wheat meat," it gets a bum rap because it is made from wheat gluten. But if you aren't celiac and do not have a wheat allergy or gluten sensitivity, it's pretty amazing. In addition to its high protein content, seitan has a substantial texture that allows it to be used as a vegan meat substitute (I provide a simple from-scratch seitan recipe on page 131.)

Nuts and seeds (sunflower, pumpkin, chia, hemp, etc.) are also excellent sources of protein: per 1-ounce serving, almonds and pistachios each offer 6 grams, cashews 5 grams, and walnuts and pecans 2.5 grams. They also contain fiber, vitamin E, magnesium, and a host of antioxidants. Some studies suggest that one to two servings of nuts per day could help reduce LDL cholesterol (the bad one) and reduce the risk of heart disease.

So just how much of each plant-based food should you eat to achieve your nutrition goals? As always, I turn to my friend Virginia Messina's "Plant Plate" from our book *Vegan for Her* and suggest you aim for the following each day:

- 3 or more servings of legumes
- 1 to 2 servings of nuts and seeds
- 4 or more servings of grains and starches
- 5 or more servings of vegetables
- 3 or more servings of fruit

My Top 10 Protein Sources

FOOD AND SERVING SIZE	PROTEIN CONTENT (G)
Seitan (3 oz)	20
Edamame (½ cup)	16
Tempeh (½ cup)	15
Bean-based pasta (2 oz)	14
Tofu (½ cup)	10
Soy curls (1 cup)	10
Peanuts (¼ cup)	9
Lentils (½ cup)	9
Black beans (½ cup)	8
Chia seeds (2 tbsp)	6

Fat Facts

Let's chew the fat. Good fat, that is. There's a lot of hype about low- and no-fat diets, but the reality is that healthy fats are important in a vegan diet. I know this because of my long-term work with Virginia Messina, who coauthored *Vegan for Life* with Jack Norris. Mono- and polyunsaturated fats are heart healthy because they improve the ratio of LDL to HDL cholesterol. Good sources of monounsaturated fatty acids are olives and olive oil, avocados, most nuts, and peanuts and peanut oil. Sources of polyunsaturated omega-3 and omega-6 fatty acids include walnuts; soybeans and soybean oil; kidney beans; seaweed (including nori); sunflower, pumpkin, flax, hemp, and chia seeds (and their oils); and canola oil. To make sure you hit your recommended daily allowance of alpha-linolenic acid, a particular type of omega-3, add one of these to your daily diet:

- 1 tablespoon walnut or canola oil
- 1 teaspoon flaxseed oil
- 2 teaspoons hempseed oil

- 1 tablespoon ground flaxseeds
- 1½ teaspoons chia seeds
- 5 walnut halves
- ⅜ cup soynuts
- 3 sheets nori seaweed

Avoid saturated fats, which are found primarily in meat, eggs, fish, and dairy, and trans fats, which are found in fried and processed foods (look for the words "hydrogenated" and "partially hydrogenated" on food labels). Both of these fats can raise "bad" cholesterol (LDL) and lower "good" cholesterol (HDL), a double whammy for bad health. Most plant-based foods are naturally low in saturated fats. Coconut oil, which is over 80 percent saturated fat, is an exception. Although it can be useful in baking, I rarely use it and I don't call for it in this book.

Bottom line: Good fats are a good part of a good vegan diet.

Veggies Are Versatile

When I went vegetarian, and later vegan, vegetables blew me away. Sounds a little ridiculous, right? But here's the thing: I had been in a meat and starch rut most of my life, and vegetables were just an afterthought on the side. Then suddenly, vegetables became the star of the show and, oh my, such variety!

Depending upon where you live, the availability of some vegetables will change with the seasons, but there are many you can find year-round that will contribute great flavor and texture to your dishes. Here are my veggie staples:

Broccoli: Perfect in stir-fries, soups, and casseroles, it's also great raw. Dip florets in hummus or vegan ranch and add chopped broccoli to salads.

Cabbage: This vitamin- and mineral-rich vegetable is healthy and available in many varieties, including green, red, savoy, napa, and bok choy. Use it in hearty roasted recipes, add it to soups, and enjoy it raw in salads.

Carrots: This naturally sweet veggie is a go-to for roasting, braising, and steaming. Mash them with russet potatoes for vibrant color and added beta-carotene. Bonus: They are an integral part of the mirepoix trifecta—chopped onion, carrot, and celery—the sautéed flavor base for so many delicious meals.

Corn: Freshly picked and steamed corn on the cob screams summer, and frozen and canned corn bring brightness and flavor to meals at a low cost. Purée corn into soups for added creaminess, stir into chili for a pop of color, or simply toss with a salad or combine with black beans for vegan taco meat.

Cauliflower: This tasty cruciferous vegetable has become the latest "it" vegetable, whether cut into "steaks" and roasted, or thrown into the food processor to create a veggie alternative to rice. You can also steam, stir-fry, braise, or enjoy it raw.

Kale: I'm cuckoo for this leafy green. It holds up to steaming (no soggy greens), and when you stir it into soup or a pot of beans, you add a healthy dose of nutrients along with color and texture. And raw? It can be a marvel if you take some time to massage it (see Avocado-Citrus Kale Salad, page 21).

Mushrooms: Meaty in texture (see discussion of umami, page 9), mushrooms can be served in a breakfast omelet, stuffed as an appetizer, or stand in for meat in soups and sandwiches. They contain B vitamins as well as antioxidants and minerals such as copper, zinc, and potassium. Common varieties include cremini (as well as baby bellas and portobellos, which are creminis allowed to grow larger), shiitake, oyster, and white button.

Onion: Oh, how I love onions! I always have several varieties on hand: sweet, yellow, white, red, and green. Low in calories, high in vitamins, minerals, and antioxidants, they pack an incredible amount of flavor, not to mention umami when you caramelize or roast them. I often say that if you don't know what to cook, start with a little olive oil and onion in a skillet and let the aroma inspire you.

Making Half-Moon Onion Slices

I call for these in several recipes. To make them, cut the whole onion in half, lengthwise, then peel. Place each half flat side down. Following the fiber line in the onion, slice to create half-moon pieces.

Potatoes: I eat potatoes and sweet potatoes almost every day. Once spurned as a "bad starch," nutrient-rich spuds can be cooked and served so many ways: baked, boiled, steamed, or fried and whole, chopped, mashed, and more. They're a good source of B and C vitamins, potassium (one serving contains more than a banana), and fiber.

Squash: There's winter squash and summer squash. I'm definitely on Team Winter, but over the years, I've learned to love both and how to use them effectively. Summer

SIMPLE STORAGE

There is nothing more frustrating than purchasing a big basket of colorful fruits and vegetables only to lose them to spoilage. The first way to avoid this is to shop with a list and try to not over-buy. Second, observe the science of food storage and follow these tips:

STORE AT ROOM TEMPERATURE:

- Bananas
- Cucumber
- Garlic
- Onion
- Oranges
- Potatoes
- Sweet potatoes
- Winter squash

STORE AT ROOM TEMPERATURE, *then move to the refrigerator when ripe:*

- Avocados
- Melons
- Pears

STORE IN THE REFRIGERATOR:

- Apples
- Asparagus
- Blueberries
- Broccoli
- Brussels sprouts
- Cabbage
- Cauliflower
- Corn (whole ears)
- Dark leafy greens
- Lemons
- Limes
- Lettuce
- Strawberries
- Summer squash

A note on herbs: Wash fresh herbs in cool water and dry. (I use a square box colander that sits over the sink.) Once dry, wrap the herbs in a paper towel and store in the refrigerator. If you want to make them last beyond a couple of days, trim an inch off the stems and set them in a mason jar with water (think bouquet of flowers) in the refrigerator. The one exception is basil, which should be stored at room temperature. Trim it and store in a jar of water on the counter and cut the leaves as you need them.

Freeze herbs that you might not be able to use in time. Blanch them (submerge in boiling water for one minute and then transfer to ice water immediately; this will preserve their color), then allow to fully dry before wrapping them in a paper towel and placing in a plastic bag and storing in the freezer for up to a year.

squash such as yellow squash and zucchini are terrific grilled and in stir-fries, but I really fell for them when I began to spiralize them into alt-noodles. Winter squash such as butternut, kabocha, and acorn can be cubed and roasted with the skin on. Even better, bake them, scoop out the flesh, and mix with veggies for a colorful stuffed squash.

Tomatoes: We all know summer is the time to best enjoy tomatoes, but I use them year-round. Hearty beefsteak tomatoes are terrific on a sandwich or wrap, sweet heirloom tomatoes can be chopped for a salad or drizzled with balsamic vinegar for an appetizer, and I'll use any kind of tomato for a homemade marinara sauce (page 129), or simply sliced and salted.

Curbing Your Carbs

Raise your hand if you considered yourself a high-carb vegan when you first started this journey (both of my hands are waving in the air). The more I got immersed in the food world, I realized that carbs were getting lumped into one category: bad. But the truth is that not all carbs are created equal. Less nutritious carbs are the simple, refined ones, such as sweetened beverages and fruit juices, white bread and pasta, pastries, and white rice—you get the idea. Complex carbs such as whole fruit, legumes, potatoes, and whole grains offer fiber and nutrients. And you can use them to replace carbohydrates that are more processed. Here are some of my favorite substitutions:

Healthy Carb Swaps

FOOD	CARBS (G)	SWAP	CARBS (G)
1 cup cooked spaghetti	43	1 cup cooked zucchini noodles	7
½ cup cooked brown rice	16	1 cup cauliflower rice	2
Flour tortilla (1)	24	Lettuce wraps (2)	2
Crackers (6)	17	Cucumber slices (6)	2
Hamburger bun (1)	29	Portobello mushroom caps (2)	1

TIME-SAVING VEGGIE PREP

This book is designed to help you get meals on the table quickly and easily. Because it's also a vegan cookbook, we're cooking with lots of vegetables for nutrition and flavor, which means lots of chopping and dicing. Fortunately, you can do much of it in advance. Just store the vegetables in an airtight container and scoop out what you need. (Not into slicing and dicing? Check out my shortcut in Basics of Speed Cooking, page 10.) You can also wash your leafy greens in advance, then pat dry, wrap in a paper towel, and store in the refrigerator.

Here are the ways I'll be asking you to prep your vegetables:

Coarsely chop: When size is less important due to the chosen cooking method (blending, pressure cooking, etc.), you just want some consistently sized pieces; aim for about 1 inch.

Chop: This is the most common vegetable prep instruction in this book. Aim for roughly ½-inch cubes.

Dice: Think of this as a smaller chop: about ¼-inch cubes.

Finely diced: These are tinier pieces, often used for garnish when you want a mini-burst of flavor.

Minced: Mostly for garlic, the pieces are very small, barely ⅛ inch. (If you buy jarred garlic, you won't have to bother with this at all.)

Grated (shredded): If it has multiple size holes, a box grater can take care of grating vegetables, shredding vegan cheese, and even mincing ginger and zesting citrus if it has a "fine shred" or "zest" blade. (If not, you may want a Microplane zester, too.)

Spiralized: For "zoodles" (zucchini noodles) and other veggie noodles, use a spiralizer. Simply place the vegetable in the device (slice a flat end to face the blade) and turn the crank. You can also use a knife or vegetable peeler to slice vegetables into ribbons.

BASICS THAT BUILD FLAVOR

I have a secret. One single element is the key to flavorful vegan cooking: umami.

Often referred to as the "fifth flavor," it brings a savory quality to food, and I try to incorporate it into all of my savory seasoning techniques, cooking methods, and flavor profiles.

Certain foods and cooking techniques bring out umami, adding a mysterious "wow" to a dish. Vegan foods with built-in umami include ripe tomatoes, mushrooms (dried and fresh),

fermented foods (such as tempeh, sauerkraut, miso, and soy sauce), wine, and nutritional yeast. (If nutritional yeast is new to you, start small—buy a cup or two from the bulk section of your local natural market.) Cooking techniques that enhance and create umami include caramelizing, roasting, grilling, and braising.

Why is umami important in vegan cooking? It brings a savory depth to foods, making them more enjoyable, and even increases feelings of satiety (fullness).

Here are some ways you can achieve incredibly flavorful, umami-rich plant-based meals:

- Build up your spice rack with these ingredients: chile powders (especially chipotle, and smoked and sweet Spanish paprika), dried mushroom powder, vegan Worcestershire sauce, soy sauce, chili sauces, and liquid smoke.

- Use flavored vegetable broths, such as beef-style, chicken-style, and curry broths—in the form of boxed or canned liquids, bouillon cubes, or powdered broth. I use Better than Bouillon, Edward and Sons, and Massel brands. I call for beef- and chicken-style broth when I think it makes sense for the flavor profile, but you can always just use whatever vegetable broth you have on hand. For those of you who are using little to no oil in your cooking, these seasoned broths are fantastic for "sautéing" your mirepoix and other vegetables. I have an Everyday Vegetable Broth recipe (Page 122) for you in chapter 8. Feel free to use it in any recipe that calls for vegetable broth.

- Begin your dish by sautéing. Some people get annoyed when recipes call for a sauté step. (Let's dump it and "set it and forget it," right?). I only ask you to sauté for about three minutes. Over high heat, and with a little bit of olive oil, you'll lightly brown the vegetables, which adds a lot of flavor. (Oil-free cooks, use seasoned vegetable broth or water.)

- Just a little bit of salt can reduce the bitterness of some ingredients while enhancing the umami elements of others.
- Acids are your friend. Lemon or lime juice is a great way to finish raw vegetables, salads, steamed greens, and cooked beans, giving them a piquant spark. And to really build up the umami in your pantry, become a vinegar collector. From balsamic to apple cider vinegar, from rice to red or white wine vinegar, this pantry staple will help you brighten almost any dish.
- Fermented foods embody umami: tempeh, sauerkraut, kimchi, pickles, and miso paste are particularly great ways to build flavor in vegan cooking.
- Very ripe tomatoes (fresh, canned, or jarred) are a simple way to add flavor to zoodles, sauces, and dressings.
- Ground dried mushrooms can add tremendous depth of flavor. Sliced fresh mushrooms sautéed or simmered with a little soy or chili sauce add meaty texture and flavor.

BASICS OF SPEED COOKING

My number one tip for fast food prep? Plan ahead. What recipes are you making this week? Plan your shopping list accordingly and then look for possible shortcuts.

- Pick up pre-diced vegetables in the produce section, or bagged in the frozen aisle.
- Buy canned beans.
- Or, buy dried beans in bulk and soak them overnight (or for eight hours) as soon as you get home. Cook them and store them in 1½-cup servings (equivalent to one 15-ounce can) in the refrigerator for up to 5 days or in the freezer for up to 3 months.
- Buy precooked grains.
  Or, when you're cooking grains, make a double portion and freeze for up to 3 months.
- Frozen vegetables such as cauliflower, broccoli, corn, and green beans are really handy to have in your freezer.
- Do you hate cutting onions or peeling and mincing garlic? You can find the Dorot Gardens brand of sautéed onions and crushed garlic (as well as other herbs) in the frozen foods section at Albertsons, Kroger, Target, Trader Joe's, Walmart, Whole Foods, and other grocers. You can also buy jarred minced garlic (my personal go-to), which is why you'll see me call for teaspoons of garlic in the recipes to make it easier for you. One teaspoon of minced garlic = one large clove of garlic.
- I love tomato paste, but sometimes just a little bit is all I need. Rather than waste the rest of the can, I buy concentrated tomato paste in tubes, which allows me to squeeze out exactly what I need, then screw the cap back on and return to the fridge. You'll find the tubes next to the cans of tomato sauce and paste at the supermarket. Tomato powder is another great option (brands include Knorr, Spice House, and Augason Farms). For tomato paste, mix 2 parts powder to 1 part water; for tomato sauce, mix 1 part powder to 6 parts water.

- I begin many recipes with mirepoix, a mix of diced onions, carrots, and celery sautéed in olive oil or cooked in vegetable broth. To make this a bit easier, I often make a big batch and then freeze 1-cup portions in small plastic bags. A classic mirepoix follows a 2:1:1 ratio, e.g. 1 cup diced onion, ½ cup diced carrot, and ½ cup diced celery. Many cuisines have similar flavor-building bases: in Italy it's called *battuto* or *soffritto* and can also include garlic, fennel, and parsley; in Spain it's *sofrito* and the celery and carrot get swapped out for bell peppers, tomatoes, and garlic. In Louisiana, you'll find the "Holy Trinity" as the base for most Creole and Cajun dishes–onions, bell peppers, and celery. All are wonderful to have in the freezer, ready to turn a can of beans into a fast, flavorful meal.

HELPFUL KITCHEN EQUIPMENT

It's almost time to get cooking, but let's first make sure you have what you need.

Must-haves:

- A 12-inch skillet, ideally one that is oven-safe. I personally love cast iron skillets.
- A large saucepan or stockpot. If you want just one, opt for a 6- or 8-quart stockpot.
- A large sheet pan; 18 by 13 inches is ideal for a standard oven and average kitchen size. Be sure it has a 1-inch rim. If you have a smaller oven or use a large toaster oven, opt for a 9-by-13-inch pan.
- A basic 8-inch square pan with 2-inch sides is great for both desserts (brownies!) and casseroles.
- A 5- to 7-quart covered casserole dish or Dutch oven. Again, I love the cast iron option, but it's simply a preference.
- A food processor and/or blender. These are helpful in a vegan kitchen to create plant-based cheeses, sauces, and dressings. Many food processors can do double duty as a blender. Wide blenders can stand in for a food processor. Ninja makes a blending system that includes a blender, food processor,

IF YOU DON'T HAVE A PRESSURE COOKER

I understand that some people don't own a pressure cooker, so in chapter 7, I provide alternate cooking options. In general, here's how to adapt a pressure cooker recipe for the stovetop: Follow the recipe until it's time to set up for pressure cooking. Here you'll bring the food up to a boil, cover, reduce the heat to simmer, and cook until done, usually three times longer than the pressure-cooking time—but you'll want to check that the food is fully cooked. You may need more water, so keep an eye on that. When a recipe calls for dried beans, opt for canned beans (for one cup of dried beans opt for two cans of beans) and reduce the liquid by 1½ cups, adding more later if needed.

and even spiralizing blades (for those zucchini noodles), all on one base. It's one of my own most-used appliances.

Optional:

- A pressure cooker (stovetop or electric) or multicooker with a pressure cooker function, such as the Instant Pot®. If you want to make full use of this book, it's really not optional because chapter 7 is dedicated to recipes for the pressure cooker. I truly believe the pressure cooker is a vegan's best friend! Cooking beans in minutes instead of hours is a game changer. Throughout the book, where appropriate, I provide "Make It Even Faster" tips that often include pressure cooker directions.
- A spiralizer for zoodles. It also works great on potatoes and cucumbers, making fried spuds and salads more fun and less effort.

HOW TO USE THIS BOOK

It's time to get cooking, so let's review how the recipes are laid out so that you know what to expect. Each recipe includes anticipated prep and cook time, dietary labels—whether the recipe is gluten-free, nut-free, soy-free, and/or oil-free—and tips.

Those tips include:

Ingredient Tip: Learn a little bit more about what you're cooking

Substitution Tip: Ingredient alternatives when you're out of stock or dislike what is called for, or want to change the recipe up to suit a dietary need

Make It Ahead: Suggestions for getting ingredients (or even the whole dish) ready earlier in the week to make weeknight cooking simpler

Make It Slower: Stovetop cooking instructions for the chapter 7 pressure cooker recipes

Make It Even Faster: Shortcuts that will decrease prep and/or cook time, including pressure cooker directions where appropriate for recipes not in chapter 7

Add Even More Protein: Turn a salad or side into something more substantial

In addition, you'll find two recipe indexes at the end of book. One is an alphabetical recipe chart that indicates dietary labels (gluten-free, nut-free, soy-free, and oil-free). Note that this means the recipe is either free of the indicated allergen or I provide an optional way to prepare the recipe without it. If you're nut free, choose plant-based milks without nuts; if you are gluten free, use oat products that are certified gluten free.

The second index is categorized by meal type: breakfast, salads, sandwiches, sides, soups, mains, and more.

Now that you know what you're in for, I think it's time to get into the kitchen for some fast and easy vegan cooking!

Avocado Not-Toast, page 31

2

No Cooking Required

Let's kick things off with quick, tasty, and healthy meals using foods that are ready to roll. Often when we're new to plant-based cuisine we think it's overly complicated and foreign. But you'll see that the ingredients we're using have likely been a part of your cooking and eating for years. Far from a "raw vegan" approach, these are simply ingredients that require no stove or oven. Through these recipes my hope is that you'll see them as a guide to get started and then begin to create meals accordingly. Start with my Super Smoothie and then move on to adding your favorite plant-based milk, fruit, and even leafy greens. Follow along with an Umami Bean Dip and soon you'll be puréeing your go-to legumes with flavors you love. This is exactly how I, at the age of 45, learned how to cook vegan!

SUPER SMOOTHIE

GLUTEN-FREE OPTION, NUT-FREE OPTION, OIL-FREE, SOY-FREE OPTION

Serves 2 / Prep time: 5 minutes

Of course I'm going to kick this cookbook off with a smoothie! It's fast *and* it's easy! This one focuses on accessible "superfoods" versus the harder to find and more expensive add-ins. Berries and nuts are packed with plant-powered nutrients. I almost always have blueberries in the freezer, but strawberries and raspberries are great, too.

1 cup unsweetened plant-based milk (any kind or Oat Milk, page 123)

1 cup blueberries (frozen or fresh)

1 banana

2 tablespoons walnuts (optional)

1 to 3 ice cubes (if using fresh blueberries)

In a blender, combine the milk, blueberries, banana, walnuts, and ice (if using). Blend until smooth.

Ingredient Tip: Soy milk and oat milk create an especially creamy smoothie.

Soy-free option: Use soy-free plant-based milk.

Gluten-free option: Use certified gluten-free oat milk.

Nut-Free option: Omit the walnuts and use soy, rice, or oat milk.

Per serving: Calories: 136; Total fat: 3g; Total carbs: 25g; Fiber: 5g; Sugar: 14g; Protein: 2g; Sodium: 181mg

AÇAI (OR NOT) BREAKFAST BOWL

GLUTEN-FREE, OIL-FREE OPTION, SOY-FREE OPTION

Serves 2 / Prep time: 5 minutes

Here's a no-frills approach to the hipster smoothie bowl. The açai berry is packed with fiber, antioxidants, and heart-healthy fats, and that's why you can find these pink bowls at juice bars and health food restaurants. We'll leave out some of the other "superfood" ingredients like seeds and green tea powders and just focus on what we usually have on hand: nut butter and fresh fruit.

2 (6-ounce) packets frozen açai berry blend (or frozen dragon fruit or 2 cups frozen berries)

2 cups unsweetened plant-based milk (any kind or Oat Milk, page 123)

2 bananas

½ cup peanut butter

¼ cup shredded unsweetened coconut or granola

1. In a blender, combine the açai and milk and purée until smooth. Pour into two serving bowls.

2. Slice one of the bananas and line the slices halfway around the edge of one of the bowls. Repeat with the second banana and bowl.

3. Spoon ¼ cup of the peanut butter into the middle of each bowl.

4. Sprinkle the coconut or granola on the other edge of each bowl.

Ingredient Tip: Dragon fruit (pitaya) is a purple alternative to açai that can cost a bit less. Or just use frozen strawberries.

Soy-free option: Use soy-free plant-based milk.

Gluten-free option: Use a gluten-free granola.

Oil-free option: Use an oil-free granola.

Per serving: Calories: 697; Total fat: 47g; Total carbs: 78g; Fiber: 18g; Sugar: 40g; Protein: 26g; Sodium: 383mg

AWESOME OVERNIGHT OATS

GLUTEN-FREE OPTION, NUT-FREE OPTION, OIL-FREE, SOY-FREE OPTION

Serves 2 / Prep time: 5 minutes

Sometimes we just don't have the time to make a hot breakfast. Overnight oats are a great way to eat a wholesome morning meal with very little effort and no cooking. Great when planning ahead, these can be set up early in the week and enjoyed within three days, right out of the refrigerator. Chia seeds help create an oatmeal-like texture but, reminiscent of tapioca, they aren't for everyone. Just skip 'em if they aren't your thing.

1 cup rolled oats

2 cups unsweetened plant-based milk (any kind or Oat Milk, page 123)

1 banana, mashed

2 tablespoons chia seeds

1. Line up two jars or containers. In one jar or container, combine ½ cup oats, 1 cup milk, half of the mashed banana, and 1 tablespoon chia seeds. Repeat in the second jar or container. Stir well (or put the lid on the jar and shake). Refrigerate overnight.

2. When serving, add additional milk, if needed.

Ingredient Tip: Dried fruit (raisins, cranberries, cherries, etc.), fresh fruit, and chopped walnuts or pecans are great additions for flavor, texture, and extra nutrients.

Soy-free option: Use soy-free plant-based milk.

Gluten-free option: Use certified gluten-free oats and/or oat milk.

Nut-free option: Use a nut-free plant-based milk.

Per serving: Calories: 375; Total fat: 14g; Total carbs: 52g; Fiber: 13g; Sugar: 8g; Protein: 11g; Sodium: 365mg

FRUIT AND VEGGIE GAZPACHO

GLUTEN-FREE, NUT-FREE, OIL-FREE, SOY-FREE OPTION

Serves 4 / Prep time: 10 minutes

Gazpacho is a cold, vegetable-based soup. Refreshing and cooling during hot summer months, it's even more so when you add seasonal watermelon. In addition, the watermelon gives us all the liquid we need in this soup.

2 large tomatoes, quartered

1 cayenne pepper, seeded and chopped

4 cups cubed fresh watermelon, divided

1 poblano pepper, seeded and chopped

1 small red onion, quartered

1 large cucumber, peeled, seeded, and coarsely chopped

¼ cup plus 2 tablespoons minced fresh dill, divided

2 teaspoons white wine vinegar

½ teaspoon salt

½ teaspoon black pepper

1. Into a food processor or blender, place the tomatoes, cayenne, and 2 cups of the watermelon. Blend until puréed, about 20 seconds.

2. Add the poblano, onion, cucumber, ¼ cup of the dill, the vinegar, salt, and pepper, and purée until smooth, about 30 seconds.

3. Divide the remaining 2 cups watermelon between four large soup bowls. Pour the soup from the processor or blender into each of the bowls. Garnish each bowl with 1½ teaspoons minced fresh dill.

Ingredient Tip: Believe it or not, hot peppers are actually quite cooling to the human body, and the cayenne pepper is what makes the flavor of this soup so special *and* cooling. Try jalapeño for a milder option. To go extra hot, try habanero or Thai pepper. If mild is more your style, try a bell pepper (any color) or ancho or peperoncini peppers.

Make It Ahead: This can be prepared up to 3 days in advance; refrigerate in an airtight container.

Add Even More Protein: If you have access to vegan feta (brands include Violife, Heidi Ho, and Vtopian), add this or a dollop of Ch-ofu Ricotta (Page 125) to the soup for a heartier meal.

Soy-free option: Avoid soy-based vegan feta cheese (if using).

Per serving: Calories: 75; Total fat: 0g; Total carbs: 18g; Fiber: 3g; Sugar: 13g; Protein: 2g; Sodium: 299mg

FIVE-FRUIT SALAD

GLUTEN-FREE, NUT-FREE, OIL-FREE, SOY-FREE OPTION

Serves 4 / Prep time: 10 minutes

Here's another make-ahead recipe I like to prepare over the weekend. I usually buy fruit that looks good at the store (sometimes precut) and whip up a quick salad. I use it as a topping for my Awesome Overnight Oats (page 18) or pack it as a snack to take to the office. For this recipe, I'm using fruit that you can almost always find year-round.

2 cups strawberries, hulled and halved

2 cups blueberries

1 cup grapes, halved

1 banana, sliced

1 large apple, cored and diced

1 tablespoon lemon juice

1 cup plain vegan yogurt (optional)

Combine all of the ingredients in a large bowl and serve.

Ingredient Tip: I've used frozen fruit for this salad and it works great! Just combine everything as listed above and it will thaw when stored in the refrigerator.

Make It Ahead: This can be prepared up to 4 days in advance; refrigerate in an airtight container.

Soy-free option: If using the yogurt, opt for almond or coconut milk yogurt.

Per serving: Calories: 136; Total fat: 1g; Total carbs: 35g; Fiber: 6g; Sugar: 24g; Protein: 2g; Sodium: 3mg

AVOCADO-CITRUS KALE SALAD

GLUTEN-FREE, NUT-FREE, OIL-FREE, SOY-FREE

Serves 4 / Prep time: 10 minutes

Kale salads are packed with nutrition and offer a great texture alternative to lettuce. Kale deserves some love and affection, and all it takes is a gentle massage to break it down and make it easier to eat. If you're not a fan of raw kale, this technique might change your mind. Really! You'll notice as you massage the leaves that the volume reduces (sometimes nearly in half) and the color becomes a deep green. Add the hemp seeds for a texture similar to Parmesan. If you want more protein, chickpeas are a perfect addition.

¼ cup dried cherries (or other dried fruit)

¼ cup orange or lemon juice

12 ounces kale

1 ripe avocado

¼ cup hemp seeds or 1 (15-ounce) can chickpeas, drained and rinsed

1. In a small bowl, place the dried cherries. Pour the juice over the cherries and allow to rehydrate for about 10 minutes.

2. De-stem and tear the kale into bite-size pieces, and place them into a large bowl. Slice the avocado in half, remove the pit, and scoop the flesh into the bowl. Add the rehydrated cherries and any excess juice. With clean or gloved hands, massage the kale until it brightens and glistens, about 3 minutes.

3. Sprinkle the hemp seeds over the salad and toss gently.

Substitution Tip: If your avocado isn't fully ripe, use 1 tablespoon avocado oil or extra-virgin olive oil instead.

Prep Tip: I always keep powder-free nitrile gloves on hand (you can find them at your local pharmacy). They are perfect to wear when massaging a salad like this (or when deseeding and chopping a jalapeño or other hot pepper).

Make It Ahead: This can be prepared up to 2 days in advance; refrigerate in an airtight container.

Per serving: Calories: 243; Total fat: 14g; Total carbs: 24g; Fiber: 5g; Sugar: 7g; Protein: 9g; Sodium: 40mg

ARTICHOKE HEART SALAD

GLUTEN-FREE, NUT-FREE, OIL-FREE, SOY-FREE

Serves 4 / Prep time: 10 minutes

Some of my favorite restaurant meals are those that are clearly easy: just the ingredients, singing with flavor. This is a nod to the fresh salads that are abundant in Mediterranean restaurants.

1 (14-ounce) can quartered artichoke hearts, rinsed and drained

1 (12-ounce) jar roasted red peppers (packed in water), drained (but not rinsed)

1 small cucumber, peeled and diced

1 large tomato, diced

¼ cup finely chopped red onion

1 tablespoon lemon juice

1½ teaspoons dried oregano

½ teaspoon salt

½ teaspoon black pepper

1. Roughly chop the artichoke hearts. Transfer to a large bowl. Finely chop the roasted red peppers and add them to the bowl.

2. Add the cucumber, tomato, onion, lemon juice, oregano, salt, and pepper. Toss gently to mix all the vegetables and serve.

Substitution Tip: Hearts of palm are a great substitute for artichoke hearts.

Make It Ahead: This salad can be prepared 3 to 5 days in advance; refrigerate in an airtight container.

Per serving: Calories: 80; Total fat: 0g; Total carbs: 16g; Fiber: 7g; Sugar: 6g; Protein: 4g; Sodium: 707mg

EGG-Y SALAD

GLUTEN-FREE, NUT-FREE

Serves 4 / Prep time: 10 minutes

Tofu is a great stand-in for egg salad because the texture and color are so similar to the classic recipe we remember. The addition of turmeric—a yellow spice—brings in the yolk color. Black salt (which is actually sometimes grayish pink) contains sulfuric compounds that lend a pleasant eggy flavor. Serve this mixture over chopped lettuce for a salad, on bread or tortillas for a sandwich or wrap, or with crackers for a snack.

1 (14-ounce) package extra-firm tofu, pressed and drained

½ cup chopped celery

½ cup chopped onion

½ cup vegan mayonnaise

½ teaspoon unseasoned rice vinegar

½ teaspoon turmeric

½ teaspoon black salt or sea salt

¼ teaspoon black pepper

1. Into a food processor or a large bowl, place all of the ingredients. *If using a food processor:* Pulse until chunky (but not puréed). *If using a bowl:* Use a potato masher or wooden spoon to crumble the tofu while combining all ingredients.

2. Refrigerate in an airtight container for an hour before serving.

Ingredient Tip: Black salt—*kala namak*—used to be a fairly exotic ingredient. When I lived in New York I had to seek out Asian and Indian markets to find it. These days you can find it on Amazon and at Walmart. It's a great addition to your plant-based pantry.

Make It Ahead: This can be prepared up to 5 days in advance.

Per serving: Calories: 149; Total fat: 11g; Total carbs: 6g; Fiber: 2g; Sugar: 1g; Protein: 8g; Sodium: 477mg

HOW TO PRESS WATER-PACKED TOFU

This is the first of many times I will call for pressed and drained tofu. Here are the basics:

1. Open the tofu package and drain the water.
2. Place a clean, lint-free dish towel or paper towels on a baking sheet.
3. Put the block of tofu on top of the towel(s) and wrap to cover the tofu.
4. Place a heavy pot on top of the wrapped tofu block to press the water out.
5. Allow the tofu to drain for 10 to 20 minutes.

You can also invest in a tofu press and let it do the work for you. Brands I use include TofuXpress, EZ Tofu Press, and Tofuture.

WHITE BEAN PESTO SALAD

GLUTEN-FREE, OIL-FREE OPTION, SOY-FREE

Serves 4 / Prep time: 15 minutes

This is a super-fresh way to enjoy an anything-but-basic bean salad. We'll start with a vegan version of pesto (no Parmesan) and simply toss it with beans and greens. Bonus: Use this pesto as a pizza sauce, sandwich spread, salad dressing, or vegetable dip.

FOR THE PESTO:

3 ounces (3 loosely packed cups) fresh basil leaves

3 ounces (4 loosely packed cups) arugula

½ cup walnuts

3 tablespoons lemon juice (about 1 large lemon)

2 tablespoons nutritional yeast

1 tablespoon minced garlic (3 cloves)

½ teaspoon salt

¼ teaspoon black pepper

1 to 2 teaspoons olive oil (or water)

FOR THE SALAD:

16 ounces baby spinach

1 (15.5-ounce) can white beans (any kind), drained and rinsed

1 large yellow bell pepper, seeded and cut into thin strips

1 cup cherry tomatoes, halved

To make the pesto: In a food processor, combine the basil, arugula, walnuts, lemon juice, nutritional yeast, garlic, salt, and pepper. Pulse until combined, creating a thick texture. Add 1 teaspoon of olive oil (or water) and blend. Add more oil (or water), if necessary, to create a paste.

To make the salad: In a large bowl, combine the spinach, beans, bell pepper, and tomatoes. Scrape the pesto into the bowl and toss gently to coat.

Make It Ahead: The pesto can be prepared up to 5 days in advance; refrigerate in an airtight container.

Oil-free option: Omit the oil.

Per serving: Calories: 316; Total fat: 12g; Total carbs: 40g; Fiber: 17g; Sugar: 5g; Protein: 19g; Sodium: 395mg

NO-CHICKEN PECAN SALAD

GLUTEN-FREE, NUT-FREE OPTION

Serves 8 / Prep time: 15 minutes

Many familiar recipes are easy to make plant-based just by using an alternative "meat," and a growing number of options are now available in mainstream grocery stores and markets. I'm a big fan of soy curls (see the Ingredient Tip below) because they are nutritious and minimally processed. No soy curls? Try your favorite brand of chicken-less strips (I like Gardein and Simple Truth); you'll need 2 (10-ounce) bags for this recipe. This is also still plenty tasty without the pecans, if you want to omit them. Serve this over lettuce for a substantial salad or wrapped in individual lettuce leaves.

1 (8-ounce) package soy curls

4 cups warm water

1 teaspoon poultry seasoning (or ½ teaspoon each ground thyme and sage)

1 large celery stalk, chopped

1 cup vegan mayonnaise (or Simple Vegan Sour Cream, page 124)

¼ cup chopped pecans

1. In a large bowl, combine the soy curls and warm water. Set aside for 10 minutes. Drain (but don't rinse) and return them to the bowl.

2. Sprinkle the soy curls with the poultry seasoning and stir to coat. Add the celery, vegan mayonnaise, and pecans and stir gently to coat. Serve immediately or cover and refrigerate for an hour or so before serving.

Ingredient Tip: My ode to the soy curl: Butler Foods, a small, family-owned business, makes a non-GMO, organic soy product using two ingredients: soybeans and spring water. The dehydrated soy curls plump up to a meaty consistency simply by soaking in warm water or broth. They are a low-calorie, protein-rich (10 grams per serving), vegan meat alternative that works in salads, soups, taco filling, stir-fries, and more. They can be ordered online and can be found in health food stores, co-ops, and the grocery chain Natural Grocers. Because they are minimally processed, be sure to store the bags of dried soy curls in the refrigerator or freezer.

Make It Ahead: This can be prepared up to 5 days in advance; refrigerate in an airtight container.

Nut-free option: Omit the pecans.

Per serving: Calories: 208; Total fat: 12g; Total carbs: 6g; Fiber: 6g; Sugar: 0g; Protein: 14g; Sodium: 226mg

THREE-BEAN BONANZA

GLUTEN-FREE, NUT-FREE, OIL-FREE OPTION, SOY-FREE

Serves 4 / Prep time: 10 minutes

You're about to make a big bowl of something good: beans! New plant-based eaters often get tripped up on beans. I certainly did because they hadn't been a big part of my pre-vegan diet. Once I realized there were so many varieties and ways to use them (puréed into a dip or made into veggie patties) I was hooked. But let's not forget that they are awesome right out of the can. For this salad, I'm using beans that my non-veg parents always have on hand. This is the first thing I make when I get to their house. Beans for days!

1 (15-ounce) can chickpeas, drained and rinsed

1 (15-ounce) can kidney beans (red, dark red, light, or white), drained and rinsed

1 (14.5-ounce) can green beans, drained and rinsed

1 small yellow or sweet onion, diced

¼ cup vinegar (apple cider or rice)

2 tablespoons olive oil (optional)

½ to 1 teaspoon salt

½ teaspoon red pepper flakes

In a large bowl, combine all the ingredients (including salt to taste) and toss until well mixed and coated.

Ingredient Tip: You can also use dried beans prepared at home (use 1½ cups each cooked chickpeas and kidney beans) and frozen or fresh (raw) green beans.

Make It Ahead: This can be prepared up to 5 days in advance; refrigerate in an airtight container.

Oil-free option: Omit the oil.

Per serving: Calories: 300; Total fat: 3g; Total carbs: 53g; Fiber: 17g; Sugar: 7g; Protein: 17g; Sodium: 306mg

UMAMI BEAN DIP

GLUTEN-FREE, NUT-FREE, OIL-FREE OPTION, SOY-FREE

Makes about 1½ cups / Prep time: 5 minutes

Every single weekend when batch cooking, I grab one can of beans—any variety is fine—and follow this process to create a dip. It's perfect for snacking on with raw vegetables or crackers, or wrapping with tortillas or lettuce. I've waxed poetic about umami (page 9), so I'm sure there's no surprise that with this recipe I'm coaching you to consider which flavors you love and how to use the ingredients you have on hand. Have fun with this one.

1 (14.5-ounce) can beans, rinsed and drained

¼ cup umami ingredient such as: sun-dried tomatoes, pitted green olives, or marinated mushrooms

2 teaspoons minced garlic (2 cloves)

½ teaspoon salt

1 to 2 tablespoons acidic liquid such as: lemon juice, lime juice, orange juice, rice vinegar, or tomato juice

1. In a food processor bowl, combine the beans, umami ingredient, garlic, and salt. Pulse until coarsely chopped.

2. With the food processor running, slowly drizzle in 1 tablespoon of the acidic liquid and process until the dip becomes creamy, adding more liquid if necessary.

Ingredient Tip: My favorite bean dip to bring to someone's house for a dinner party begins with this recipe. I use cannellini beans (white kidney beans), oil-packed sun-dried tomatoes, and lemon juice. It's so easy but it always wows!

Make It Ahead: This can be prepared up to 5 days ahead; refrigerate in an airtight container.

Oil-free option: Choose an oil-free umami ingredient.

Per serving (¼ cup): Calories: 83; Total fat: 0g; Total carbs: 15g; Fiber: 5g; Sugar: 1g; Protein: 6g; Sodium: 243mg

AVOCADO BLACK BEAN MEDLEY

GLUTEN-FREE, NUT-FREE, OIL-FREE, SOY-FREE

Serves 2 to 4 / Prep time: 10 minutes

Whole-ingredients guacamole, anyone? Instead of mashing the standard guac ingredients, in this recipe they are left intact and combined with chopped kale to add nutrient density and texture. Add the black beans to transform it into a meal. Serve this as a salad for two or as an appetizer for four with tortilla chips or crackers.

2 cups tightly packed, finely chopped kale

1 lime, juiced

1 teaspoon minced garlic (1 clove)

½ teaspoon red pepper flakes

½ teaspoon salt

¼ teaspoon ground cumin

1 (15-ounce) can black beans, drained and rinsed (or 1½ cups cooked black beans)

2 avocados, halved, pitted, and diced

2 cups cherry tomatoes, quartered

¼ cup finely diced red onion

1. Place the chopped kale in a large bowl.

2. In a small bowl or measuring cup, whisk the lime juice, garlic, red pepper flakes, salt, and cumin together. Pour over the kale. Toss to coat (or use your hands to massage the dressing into the kale). Add the beans, avocados, tomatoes, and onion and toss gently.

Substitution Tip: Use pinto beans or corn to replace the black beans.

Per serving: Calories: 272; Total fat: 14g; Total carbs: 33g; Fiber: 14g; Sugar: 3g; Protein: 10g; Sodium: 318mg

EDAMAME PEANUT SLAW

GLUTEN-FREE OPTION, OIL-FREE, SOY-FREE OPTION

Serves 4 / Prep time: 10 minutes

You know what can make vegan non-cooking *really* fast and easy? Opting for some of the freshest ready-to-roll items at the store. Keeping prewashed and bagged vegetables from the fresh produce and frozen food sections on hand means you can make very fast meals in a pinch. Serve this as a salad or use it as a tortilla filling or in a collard green or lettuce leaf wrap.

1 (16-ounce) bag frozen shelled edamame

1 (16-ounce) bag coleslaw or shredded cabbage

½ cup peanut sauce (store-bought or use Peanut Sauce, page 130)

2 tablespoons unseasoned rice vinegar

1. Place the frozen shelled edamame in the refrigerator for 8 hours before using or pour into a bowl with hot water for about 5 minutes to thaw and then drain.

2. In a large bowl, combine the thawed edamame and coleslaw. Add the peanut sauce and vinegar and toss gently to coat.

Substitution Tip: Broccoli slaw mix is a great alternative to traditional coleslaw mix.

Make It Ahead: This dish can be prepared 3 to 5 days in advance; refrigerate in an airtight container.

Soy-free option: Use soy-free peanut sauce.

Gluten-free option: Use gluten-free tamari or soy sauce to make the peanut sauce.

Per serving: Calories: 172; Total fat: 6g; Total carbs: 17g; Fiber: 7g; Sugar: 6g; Protein: 14g; Sodium: 32mg

CUCUMBER ZOODLE BOWL

GLUTEN-FREE, NUT-FREE, OIL-FREE, SOY-FREE

Serves 4 / Prep time: 10 minutes

Get your spiralizer out! In a matter of minutes, you're going to have bright, colorful, and fun vegetables. This is a great way to get out of the salad rut while getting all of the benefits of eating fresh, raw vegetables. The dressing is intentionally simple so that you can experience the flavor and variety of textures in each bite.

2 large zucchinis, spiralized

1 large cucumber, spiralized

1 large carrot, spiralized

2 scallions, julienned

2 tablespoons unseasoned rice or white wine vinegar

½ teaspoon salt

¼ teaspoon black pepper

1. In a large bowl, combine the spiralized zucchini, cucumber, and carrot. Add the julienned scallions.

2. In a small bowl or measuring cup, whisk the vinegar, salt, and pepper together. Pour over the vegetables and toss gently.

Ingredient Tip: Here is a simple way to julienne scallions:

1. Trim the white root end and the top inch of the green end, and peel away the outer layer of the scallion.

2. Cut each scallion into about 3 pieces, about 2 inches in length.

3. Halve each piece lengthwise.

4. Placing the light, inner side down, cut lengthwise into thin, even slivers or "matchsticks."

Make It Ahead: This can be prepared up to 3 days in advance; refrigerate in an airtight container.

Per serving: Calories: 49; Total fat: 0g; Total carbs: 11g; Fiber: 3g; Sugar: 5g; Protein: 3g; Sodium: 322mg

AVOCADO NOT-TOAST

GLUTEN-FREE OPTION, NUT-FREE, OIL-FREE OPTION, SOY-FREE

Serves 2 / Prep time: 5 minutes

When the avocado toast craze hit, I was sure it would pass in no time. Nope. Restaurants now serve a piece of toast with mashed avocado and sometimes they offer a little something extra (like edible flowers, at my favorite local coffee shop). For this no-cooking version, think of it as an open-faced sandwich.

1 ripe avocado

2 slices vegan whole-grain or gluten-free bread

2 teaspoons nutritional yeast

2 teaspoons pumpkin seeds

Red pepper flakes or hot sauce (optional)

1. Cut the avocado in half and remove the pit. Scoop half of the avocado out and mash it onto a piece of bread with a fork. Mash the other half on the second piece of bread.

2. Sprinkle 1 teaspoon of nutritional yeast over each piece of bread, then 1 teaspoon of pumpkin seeds. For a little kick, sprinkle with a pinch of red pepper flakes or shake a few drops of hot sauce on each piece.

Ingredient Tip: Use a really nice bread for this, particularly since you're not toasting it. My local grocery store usually has fresh vegan loaves daily.

Gluten-free option: Use gluten-free bread.

Oil-free option: Use bread without added oil.

Per serving: Calories: 289; Total fat: 17g; Total carbs: 27g; Fiber: 12g; Sugar: 2g; Protein: 14g; Sodium: 145mg

MARINATED MUSHROOM SANDWICH

GLUTEN-FREE OPTION, NUT-FREE, SOY-FREE

Serves 4 / Prep time: 10 minutes

I love this recipe because, as simple as it is, it's full of flavor. Portobello mushrooms—an umami ingredient—are thick and meaty (which is why you often see them on restaurant menus as a "burger") and absorb the marinade beautifully. You can have some fun with this one, switching up a few ingredients (swap lime juice for vinegar, avocado oil for olive oil, and dried cayenne and chipotle pepper for the basil and oregano).

3 large portobello mushroom caps

¼ cup balsamic vinegar

2 tablespoons olive oil

2 teaspoons minced garlic (2 cloves)

1 teaspoon dried basil

1 teaspoon dried oregano

¼ teaspoon salt

¼ teaspoon black pepper

8 slices vegan whole-grain bread

2 to 4 tablespoons whole-grain or Dijon mustard (optional)

1. Use a damp paper towel to wipe each mushroom clean, removing the stem if still attached. Use the tip of a spoon to gently scrape out the black gills. Cut each cap into 8 thin slices. In a shallow baking dish or baking sheet large enough to accommodate them all, lay out the mushrooms so that the slices form a single layer.

2. In a small bowl, whisk together the vinegar, olive oil, garlic, basil, oregano, salt, and pepper. Pour over the mushroom slices, tossing them gently to coat. Cover the mushrooms and refrigerate for at least 30 minutes (and up to 48 hours).

3. To assemble the sandwiches, spread 1½ teaspoons to 1 tablespoon of mustard (if using; or use hummus for more protein; see the tip below) on a slice of the bread. Lay 6 mushroom slices over the mustard, cover with a second piece of bread, and serve.

Substitution Tip: You can use a low-carb vegan tortilla or large leafy green (Swiss chard or collard greens are great) as a "wrap" to replace the bread.

Add Even More Protein: Use hummus or Umami Bean Dip (page 27) instead of mustard to make the sandwich a heartier meal.

Gluten-free option: Use gluten-free vegan bread or wraps.

Per serving: Calories: 222; Total fat: 9g; Total carbs: 27g; Fiber: 5g; Sugar: 4g; Protein: 9g; Sodium: 417mg

ANY HUMMUS WRAP

GLUTEN-FREE OPTION, NUT-FREE OPTION, OIL-FREE OPTION, SOY-FREE

Serves 4 / Prep time: 10 minutes

Hummus is a vegan cliché, but who cares? It's delicious. Traditionally, hummus is made with chickpeas, tahini, garlic, oil, and lemon juice. We're following that formula here but it's called "Any" hummus because you can use whichever bean you want, *and* you can substitute peanut butter or almond butter for the tahini.

1 (15-ounce) can beans (any kind, or 1½ cups cooked beans), rinsed and drained

1 tablespoon tahini, natural peanut butter, or almond butter

1 tablespoon lemon or lime juice (or unseasoned rice vinegar)

2 teaspoons minced garlic (2 cloves)

1 to 2 teaspoons olive oil or water

4 vegan whole-grain tortillas

4 Swiss chard or large lettuce leaves

1. In a food processor, combine the beans, tahini, lemon juice, garlic, and 1 teaspoon olive oil (or water). Purée, adding additional oil or water as needed to achieve a creamy consistency.

2. Place the tortillas on a large cutting board or counter. Spread one quarter of the hummus (about ½ cup) on each wrap. Place one Swiss chard leaf on top of the hummus. Roll and serve.

Make It Ahead: Believe it or not, you can prepare these in advance. Ideally, use two Swiss chard leaves for each wrap. Place one on top of the tortilla, then add the hummus. Place the second leaf over the hummus and roll. The chard serves as a barrier between the tortilla and the hummus, preventing a soggy wrap. Store in the refrigerator for up to two days.

Gluten-free option: Use a gluten-free tortilla or wrap.

Nut-free option: Use tahini instead of almond or peanut butter.

Oil-free option: Use water instead of oil.

Per serving: Calories: 258; Total fat: 7g; Total carbs: 41g; Fiber: 8g; Sugar: 3g; Protein: 10g; Sodium: 140mg

BURRITO LETTUCE WRAPS

GLUTEN-FREE, NUT-FREE, OIL-FREE OPTION, SOY-FREE OPTION

Serves 4 / Prep time: 15 minutes

Lettuce is a low-carb alternative to wheat and flour tortillas. Use romaine lettuce for "boats," which are easy to serve and fairly easy to eat (no shame in using a fork or knife, though). Use the marinated ingredients below, or try some of the Avocado Black Bean Medley (page 28).

1½ cups finely chopped mushrooms

2 tablespoons vegetable broth

1 tablespoon hot sauce

½ teaspoon chili powder

8 large romaine lettuce leaves

1 cup diced tomato (about 1 medium tomato)

1 cup shredded vegan cheese (optional)

½ cup diced onion

1. In a medium bowl, place the mushrooms. Add the broth, hot sauce, and chili powder, and mix well. Set aside for 5 minutes.

2. On each lettuce leaf, place ¾ cup marinated mushrooms, ¼ cup diced tomato, ¼ cup shredded vegan cheese (if using), and 2 tablespoons diced onion. Beginning with one long side, roll the lettuce leaf toward the middle to form a burrito.

Substitution Tip: Collard greens or Swiss chard leaves are excellent options to replace the romaine.

Oil-free option: Omit the vegan cheese.

Soy-free option: Use a soy-free vegan cheese.

Per serving: Calories: 26; Total fat: 0g; Total carbs: 5g; Fiber: 1g; Sugar: 3g; Protein: 2g; Sodium: 128mg

SALAD PITA PIZZA

GLUTEN-FREE OPTION, NUT-FREE, OIL-FREE OPTION, SOY-FREE

Serves 4 / Prep time: 5 minutes

Think of this as a deconstructed pita sandwich. Instead of cutting the pita and stuffing it with goodness, you're just putting everything on top to remove one step from the process. This is a really fun after-school snack, too, because it's something your kids can put together on their own. As for me? I often pack all of the elements in a container and put my pita pizza together at the office.

1 large tomato

½ cup hummus, store-bought or from the Any Hummus Wrap (page 33)

4 (6- or 8-inch) vegan pita breads

2 cups shredded lettuce

1. Slice the tomato into 4 pieces. Then cut each piece in half for 8 small pieces.

2. Spread 2 tablespoons hummus over one pita bread. Place 2 pieces of tomato on the hummus, then top with ½ cup lettuce. Repeat to make 4 pita pizzas and serve.

Substitution Tip: Try this with Umami Bean Dip (page 27) or any store-bought vegan bean dip or purée.

Oil-free option: Use oil-free hummus or bean dip.

Gluten-free option: Use vegan gluten-free pita bread.

Per serving: Calories: 234; Total fat: 5g; Total carbs: 42g; Fiber: 7g; Sugar: 2g; Protein: 9g; Sodium: 463mg

Macro Miso Soup, page 42

3

Thirty-Minute Meals (or Less)

This cookbook is designed to show you the simplicity of putting together interesting flavors with ease in vegan cooking. And that means that many of the recipes are pretty darn fast, and even the ones that take a bit of time are still simple. This chapter is about both. I want you to create depth of flavor even when pulling together a really fast meal. You'll notice I'm using quicker-cooking ingredients—sometimes the freshest of prepared foods to speed things along—as well as quicker cooking techniques. As you use this book and build your culinary muscles, many techniques may help you become a more intuitive cook.

BREAKFAST BURRITO

GLUTEN-FREE, NUT-FREE, OIL-FREE OPTION, SOY-FREE OPTION

Serves 4 / Prep time: 10 minutes / Cook time: 8 minutes

Fresh and fast, this is a toned-down burrito, but it's still loaded with flavor. It forgoes traditional potatoes, which take a long time to cook, and meat, of course. Pinto beans and leafy greens are the star of this simple, handheld breakfast (or lunch or dinner).

1 teaspoon olive oil

1 small red onion, sliced

1 (15-ounce) can pinto beans, drained and rinsed

6 ounces (4 loosely packed cups) baby spinach

1 cup fresh or jarred salsa

1 large avocado

4 vegan whole-grain or gluten-free tortillas

½ cup vegan sour cream

1. In a large skillet over medium-high heat, heat the olive oil. Add the onion and sauté until the onion begins to soften, about 3 minutes. Add the beans, spinach, and salsa and stir to mix. Cover, reduce the heat to medium-low, and simmer for 5 minutes.

2. Slice the avocado in half vertically and remove the pit. For each half, slice the avocado inside the skin, lengthwise, with the tip of a knife (try to avoid piercing the avocado skin) to create 4 slices. Scoop the slices out of the skin with a spoon.

3. On a cutting board, lay out the tortillas. Spoon about ½ cup of the beans onto each tortilla. Add 2 avocado slices and 2 tablespoons of the sour cream to each. Beginning with the side running parallel to the avocado slices, roll each of the tortillas up about halfway, fold the sides in to the middle, and continue to roll up, then serve.

Add Even More Protein: Add 1 (14-ounce) package extra-firm tofu (pressed and drained) during step 1 when you add the beans.

Soy-free option: Omit the vegan sour cream.

Oil-free option: Use 2 teaspoons water instead of the oil to sauté, and make it with Simple Vegan Sour Cream (page 124) or just omit the vegan sour cream.

Per serving: Calories: 419; Total fat: 21g; Total carbs: 48g; Fiber: 21g; Sugar: 5g; Protein: 20g; Sodium: 458mg

TOMATO TOFU SCRAMBLE

GLUTEN-FREE, NUT-FREE, OIL-FREE OPTION

Serves 4 / Prep time: 10 minutes / Cook time: 10 minutes

Tofu scramble is a staple for most vegans and many plant-based restaurants because it is nutrient dense and a hearty protein source. It's an ideal make-ahead recipe because it stores easily and, frankly, gets better after a few days in the refrigerator.

1 teaspoon olive oil

1 small yellow onion, diced

1 tablespoon minced garlic (3 cloves)

3 large stalks celery, chopped

2 large carrots, peeled (optional) and chopped

1 (14-ounce) package extra-firm tofu, pressed and drained (see page 23)

1 teaspoon turmeric

½ teaspoon dried basil

½ teaspoon dried oregano

½ teaspoon salt (optional)

¼ teaspoon black pepper

2 large tomatoes, diced

1. In a large skillet over medium-high heat, heat the olive oil. Add the onion, garlic, celery, and carrots and sauté until the onion begins to soften, about 3 minutes.

2. Crumble the tofu with your hands into the skillet (or mash with a potato masher in a medium bowl and then transfer to the skillet). Add the turmeric, basil, oregano, salt (if using), and pepper and cook, stirring a few times, for 5 more minutes.

3. Add the tomato and mix well. Cover, reduce the heat to medium-low, and cook for 2 minutes more, then serve.

Make It Ahead: This recipe calls for mirepoix (the chopped mixture of onion, garlic, celery, and carrots); this is a great cooking staple you can prepare in bulk over the weekend, then refrigerate and use as needed during the week. You can also find this mixture sold frozen at the supermarket.

Oil-free option: Use water instead of the oil to sauté.

Per serving: Calories: 137; Total fat: 7g; Total carbs: 10g; Fiber: 3g; Sugar: 4g; Protein: 11g; Sodium: 52mg

BAC'N BROCCOLI RICE SKILLET

GLUTEN-FREE OPTION, NUT-FREE, OIL-FREE OPTION

Serves 4 / Prep time: 10 minutes / Cook time: 5 minutes

Riced cauliflower is gaining popularity, but many people don't think of doing the same with broccoli. I love using it to add a pop of green to dishes, and the flavor can be a bit milder than cauliflower. Here we're combining it with smoky tempeh bacon to create a quick, comforting meal that's suitable for breakfast or any time.

1 head broccoli, cut into florets

2 (8-ounce) packages tempeh bacon

1 teaspoon olive oil

1 large red bell pepper, seeded and cut into strips

¼ teaspoon black pepper

1. Into a food processor, put the broccoli florets and pulse until chopped to look like rice (or use a knife to chop finely).

2. Cut the bacon strips into ½-inch bites.

3. In a large skillet, heat the olive oil over medium-high heat. Add the broccoli, tempeh, pepper strips, and black pepper. Sauté until the bacon begins to brown, 4 to 5 minutes, and serve.

Ingredient Tip: Make this faster by buying 1 (12-ounce) bag of frozen riced broccoli.

Gluten-free option: Use gluten-free tempeh and Worcestershire sauce, tamari, or soy sauce.

Oil-free option: Use 2 teaspoons water instead of the oil to sauté.

Per serving: Calories: 259; Total fat: 8g; Total carbs: 30g; Fiber: 11g; Sugar: 7g; Protein: 20g; Sodium: 978mg

MAKE YOUR OWN TEMPEH BACON

Combine the following ingredients in a measuring cup and pour over sliced tempeh in a shallow container or plastic bag. Cover (or seal the bag) and refrigerate overnight before using:

2 tablespoons maple syrup

1 teaspoon avocado oil or olive oil

½ teaspoon vegan Worcestershire sauce, tamari, or soy sauce

½ teaspoon cayenne pepper

⅛ teaspoon liquid smoke

FAST OATS

GLUTEN-FREE, NUT-FREE OPTION, OIL-FREE, SOY-FREE OPTION

Serves 4 / Prep time: 5 minutes / Cook time: 1 minute

In most vegan cookbooks you'll find recipes that use steel-cut and rolled oats—nice and wholesome, like the Savory Oats (page 109) in chapter 7—but this is the speedy chapter, so we're going old school with instant oats, sweet style. The recipe is rather obvious but, honestly, I think we home cooks often skip over the obvious. The purpose of this recipe is to remind you that simple oats boosted with high-protein soy milk are meal-worthy. This is gluten-free if you buy certified gluten-free oats.

2 cups sweetened, vanilla soy milk

1 cup quick (instant) oats

½ cup raisins

¼ cup chopped walnuts (optional)

1. In a medium saucepan, bring the milk to a boil. Stir in the oats, reduce the heat to medium, and cook for 1 minute.

2. Remove the pan from the heat. Sprinkle the raisins over the oatmeal. Cover and let stand for 2 to 3 minutes.

3. Serve sprinkled with 1 tablespoon chopped walnuts per serving, if using.

Substitution Tip: For savory-style quick oats, use 2 cups vegetable broth (Everyday Vegetable Broth, page 122) instead of the soy milk, skip the raisins, and consider peanuts or pistachios instead of walnuts.
Nut-free option: Omit the walnuts.
Soy-free option: Use pea milk such as Ripple, which is as high in protein as soy milk.

Per serving: Calories: 194; Total fat: 3g; Total carbs: 37g; Fiber: 4g; Sugar: 16g; Protein: 7g; Sodium: 48mg

MACRO MISO SOUP

GLUTEN-FREE OPTION, NUT-FREE, OIL-FREE

Serves 4 / Prep time: 10 minutes / Cook time: 15 minutes

My culinary career launched by accident. A friend invited me to attend a three-day cooking course with her in Philadelphia, and suddenly I was studying the macrobiotic diet with Christina Pirello, of PBS's *Christina Cooks*. With roots in Buddhism, the macrobiotic diet is designed to achieve balance in how we eat. Well, I was hooked. What's not to love about a diet rich in grains, vegetables, and soup? Learning how to make a basic miso soup is a great way to eat well and eat fast. Note that in the recipe, you whisk the miso into the broth after cooking. By doing so, you preserve the natural probiotics in the miso.

2 medium carrots, thinly sliced or chopped

½ cup sliced shiitake mushroom caps

1 teaspoon wakame flakes (optional)

1 cup cubed firm tofu

4 cups water

1 pound baby bok choy

½ cup thinly sliced scallions (with greens)

2 tablespoons miso paste (white, yellow, or red)

1 to 2 tablespoons soy sauce or tamari (optional)

1. In a large saucepan, combine the carrots, mushrooms, wakame flakes (if using), tofu, and water. Bring to a boil over medium heat. Reduce the heat to low and simmer for 10 minutes.

2. Cut the bok choy in half lengthwise and thoroughly rinse it, taking care to get the water down between the stems and leaves where dirt can get lodged. Leave small leaves whole, or cut them into pieces.

3. Remove the soup from the heat. Spoon about 1 cup of the broth into a bowl or measuring cup.

4. Transfer the bok choy and scallions to the saucepan and cover.

5. Add the miso paste to the cup of broth and whisk until dissolved. Pour the miso broth into the pot. Stir well to combine. Add soy sauce to taste (if using) before serving.

Ingredient Tip: Wakame flakes are typically found in the Asian foods section of the supermarket.

Substitution Tips: You can use 2 to 3 dried shiitakes instead of fresh; rehydrate in warm water until softened, about 15 minutes. Drain and rinse to remove any grit, then slice. Any leafy green can stand in for baby bok choy. Try collard greens (about 4 large leaves; discard the stems before cutting into pieces) or 8 ounces baby spinach (no need to cut into pieces).

Gluten-free option: Use a gluten-free soy sauce or tamari and gluten-free miso.

Per serving: Calories: 141; Total fat: 6g; Total carbs: 12g; Fiber: 4g; Sugar: 5g; Protein: 14g; Sodium: 433mg

CREAMY PORTOBELLO SOUP

GLUTEN-FREE, NUT-FREE, OIL-FREE OPTION, SOY-FREE OPTION

Serves 4 / Prep time: 10 minutes / Cook time: 15 minutes

My favorite way to make creamy vegan dishes that are also hearty enough to be a meal is to turn to my old favorite: soy milk. In this soup I'm using portobello mushrooms because the texture is so meaty, and green peas because they boast 8 grams of protein per serving. I'm a big fan of soups that offer everything you need for a complete meal.

1 teaspoon olive oil

1 small onion (sweet, yellow, or white), chopped

2 teaspoons minced garlic (2 cloves)

1 cup diced carrot

½ teaspoon dried rosemary

½ teaspoon dried sage

½ teaspoons smoked paprika

2 cups chopped portobello mushrooms (about 1 large portobello cap)

2 cups vegetable broth

2 cups unsweetened soy milk

1 cup green peas (frozen, canned, or fresh)

½ teaspoon salt

½ teaspoon pepper

1. In a large saucepan or pot, heat the olive oil over medium-high heat. Add the onion, garlic, carrot, rosemary, sage, and smoked paprika. Cook for 3 minutes, stirring a few times. Add the mushrooms and cook until the mushrooms soften, about another 2 minutes.

2. Add the broth, soy milk, peas, salt, and pepper. Bring to a boil, then immediately reduce the heat to medium-low and simmer for 10 minutes. Serve.

Ingredient Tip: You'll notice that I turn to smoked paprika in many recipes. It's an accessible and easy-to-add umami (page 9) ingredient. It gives just a bit of color to some fabulous vegan dishes that can sometimes tend to be beige. Since we eat with our eyes, color is always important. The paprika and green peas add some visual appeal to this lovely soup.

Oil-free option: Use 1 tablespoon water instead of the oil to sauté.

Soy-free option: Use a soy-free plant-based milk.

Per serving: Calories: 119; Total fat: 3g; Total carbs: 15g; Fiber: 5g; Sugar: 6g; Protein: 8g; Sodium: 613mg

SPEEDY CORN CHOWDER

GLUTEN-FREE OPTION, NUT-FREE OPTION, OIL-FREE OPTION, SOY-FREE OPTION

Serves 6 / Prep time: 10 minutes / Cook time: 20 minutes

The secret creamy ingredient for this chowder is fingerling potatoes. Not only do the potatoes create a thick texture, they cook quickly—and speed is the name of the game for this one.

2 teaspoons vegan butter (or olive oil)

1 small sweet or Vidalia onion, diced

1 pound fingerling potatoes (unpeeled)

2 cups vegetable broth

1 (16-ounce) bag frozen corn

1 cup unsweetened plant-based milk (soy, almond, cashew, or Oat Milk, page 123), divided

1 teaspoon dried oregano

1 teaspoon dried thyme

1 teaspoon salt

½ teaspoon black pepper

2 tablespoons all-purpose flour (optional)

1. In a large saucepan or pot, melt the vegan butter over medium-high heat. Add the onion and potatoes and sauté until the onions begin to soften, about 3 minutes. Add the broth and bring to a boil. Reduce the heat to low, cover, and simmer until the potatoes are tender, about 10 minutes.

2. Increase the heat to medium and stir in the corn, ½ cup of the milk, the oregano, thyme, salt, and pepper. (If you're not using flour to thicken the chowder, add the entire cup of plant-based milk).

3. If using the flour, in a small bowl, whisk it with the remaining ½ cup milk until smooth, then stir into the soup. Turn the heat back up to medium-high and cook until boiling, about 3 minutes, then serve.

Substitution Tip: Opt for 1 (15.25-ounce) can of corn (rinsed and drained) or 2 cups fresh corn to replace the frozen corn.

Gluten-free option: Use 2 teaspoons cornstarch or arrowroot instead of the all-purpose flour.

Nut-free option: Use a nut-free milk.

Soy-free option: Use a soy-free butter and milk.

Oil-free option: Use 1 tablespoon water or vegetable broth instead of the vegan butter or olive oil to sauté.

Per serving: Calories: 135; Total fat: 4g; Total carbs: 22g; Fiber: 3g; Sugar: 5g; Protein: 5g; Sodium: 707mg

EASY MINESTRONE

GLUTEN-FREE OPTION, NUT-FREE, OIL-FREE OPTION, SOY-FREE

Serves 4 / Prep time: 10 minutes / Cook time: 13 minutes

Minestrone soup has evolved over the years, but a few things remain at the heart: use whatever vegetables are on hand and include beans and pasta. This recipe will give you some freedom to get creative, while providing a solid base if you prefer simply to follow along with the measurements, using the vegetables you have.

1 teaspoon olive oil

1 cup diced onion (any kind)

½ cup diced carrot

½ cup diced celery

2 to 3 teaspoons minced garlic (2 or 3 cloves)

2 teaspoons dried basil

1 (15.5-ounce) can cannellini beans, drained and rinsed

1 (15-ounce) can tomato sauce

2 cups chicken-style vegan broth or vegetable broth

1 cup water

1 cup diced mushrooms

½ cup dried vegan ditalini pasta (see Substitution Tips, right)

½ teaspoon salt

¼ teaspoon red pepper flakes

1. In a large saucepan, heat the olive oil over medium-high heat. Add the onion, carrot, celery, and garlic and cook until the vegetables begin to soften, about 3 minutes.

2. Add the basil, beans, tomato sauce, broth, water, mushrooms, pasta, salt, and red pepper flakes, stir well, and bring to a boil. Reduce the heat to medium-low and cook, uncovered, until the pasta is tender, about 10 minutes, stirring occasionally.

Substitution Tips: If you want to get creative with this recipe, here are my suggestions:

- **Vegetables:** Use 1 cup diced zucchini; fresh, frozen, or canned green beans cut into 1-inch pieces; or any diced vegetable you love and have on hand, in place of the mushrooms.
- **Beans:** Raid your pantry for any canned white or red beans to replace the cannellini beans.
- **Pasta:** Use any small tube pasta to replace the ditalini, such as elbow, tubini, or orzo (or omit it altogether if you want a lower-carb option).

Make It Ahead: Use prepped mirepoix (see page 11) to cook this up even faster!

Oil-free option: Use 1 tablespoon water instead of the oil to sauté.

Gluten-free option: Use gluten-free pasta. This may affect cooking time in step 2. Follow the package directions.

Per serving: Calories: 244; Total fat: 3g; Total carbs: 43g; Fiber: 10g; Sugar: 8g; Protein: 15g; Sodium: 543mg

COCONUT CURRY SOUP

GLUTEN-FREE, NUT-FREE, OIL-FREE, SOY-FREE

Serves 4 / Prep time: 5 minutes / Cook time: 15 minutes

A traditional (dare I say, fancy?) culinary artist would have you make this soup in reverse: cook the food and then blend. But many of us busy home cooks don't want to fuss with spooning hot food into a blender, so I made it easier—and safer!—for us (hot liquid in a blender can expand and come through the lid). Let's blend, let's cook, and let's eat!

1½ cups vegetable broth

1 (15-ounce) can chickpeas, drained

1 large carrot, roughly chopped

1 small red onion, quartered

½ teaspoon tandoori seasoning

½ teaspoon curry powder

¼ teaspoon salt

1 (13.5-ounce) can coconut milk

⅛ to ¼ teaspoon white pepper

1. In a blender or food processor, combine the broth, chickpeas, carrot, onion, tandoori seasoning, curry powder, salt, and coconut milk and blend until smooth.

2. Transfer to a large saucepan or pot and bring to a vigorous simmer over medium-high heat (constant small bubbles will form). Reduce the heat to low and gently simmer for 10 minutes. Stir in the pepper before serving.

Ingredient Tip: Make your own tandoori seasoning! Combine equal parts paprika, ground coriander, and cayenne pepper.

Make It Even Faster: If you have a high-speed blender (such as a Vitamix or BlendTec) you can "cook" this soup in the blender! Add all of the ingredients and blend at the highest speed for 6 minutes. Voilà! Hot soup!

Per serving: Calories: 385; Total fat: 26g; Total carbs: 32g; Fiber: 9g; Sugar: 9g; Protein: 12g; Sodium: 485mg

CAULIFLOWER FRIED RICE

GLUTEN-FREE, NUT-FREE, OIL-FREE OPTION, SOY-FREE OPTION

Serves 4 / Prep time: 10 minutes / Cook time: 12 minutes

This recipe is proof that you really can make a vegan version of just about anything, and in this case a lower-carb one, too. Cauliflower rice stands in for the grain, and vegan egg—yes, it's a thing—brings it all together. Vegan eggs are now available in liquid and powder form. The following brands work for recipes like this one when you need the egg to "set": JUST Egg, Scramblit, VeganEgg by Follow Your Heart, and Vegg. You can, of course, omit the vegan egg altogether for a tasty vegetable stir-fry. We're using a food processor for this version of cauliflower rice because we want to start with raw cauliflower.

1 small (1½-pound) head cauliflower, trimmed and cut into small florets

1 teaspoon olive oil

2 teaspoons minced garlic (2 cloves)

1 cup shredded cabbage

4 scallions, diced (white and green parts kept separated)

½ teaspoon salt

2 vegan eggs (optional)

1 teaspoon chili paste

1. Into a food processor, place the cauliflower florets. Pulse until the cauliflower looks like rice, taking care not to purée it.

2. In a large skillet over medium-high heat, heat the olive oil and garlic together until the garlic is fragrant. Add the riced cauliflower and cook, stirring frequently, for about 3 minutes, then add the cabbage, the white diced scallions, and salt and cook until the cabbage is crisp-tender, another 3 minutes. If using, pour the vegan eggs into the skillet and cook without stirring for about 3 minutes. Slowly stir in the chili paste, gently combining the egg and vegetables, then serve, garnishing with the green diced scallions.

Add Even More Protein: Serve with Lentil Loaf Squares (page 78) or Barbecue Tofu (page 50) for a hearty, veggie-filled meal.

Soy-free option: Use soy-free Scramblit vegan egg or omit the vegan egg.

Oil-free Option: Use 1 tablespoon water instead of the oil to sauté.

Per serving: Calories: 42; Total fat: 2g; Total carbs: 7g; Fiber: 3g; Sugar: 3g; Protein: 2g; Sodium: 331mg

MASHED (RICED) CAULIFLOWER

GLUTEN-FREE, NUT-FREE, OIL-FREE, SOY-FREE OPTION

Serves 4 / Prep time: 10 minutes / Cook time: 20 minutes

Cauliflower rice is a culinary low-carb darling that I can actually get behind. I love this cruciferous vegetable, and whenever there's a way to add it to a meal, I'm a happy gal. I call this one "mashed" because once cooked, simply mashing with a fork or potato masher rices it immediately; no food processor required.

2 teaspoons salt, divided

1 large head cauliflower, trimmed and cut into small florets

¼ cup unsweetened plant-based milk (any kind or Oat Milk, page 123)

¼ teaspoon black pepper

1. Bring a large pot of water to a boil. Add 1 teaspoon of the salt and the cauliflower and cook until very tender, about 10 minutes. Reserve ¼ cup of the cooking liquid and then drain well.

2. Return the cauliflower to the pot over low heat. Add the milk and mash with a potato masher. Add some of the reserved cooking water, if necessary, to achieve a creamy texture. Stir in the remaining 1 teaspoon salt and the pepper, and serve.

Ingredient Tip: Add spices and seasonings to this dish based on the flavor profile of your meal. Add ¼ teaspoon curry powder and serve with the Chana Masala (page 74) or ¼ teaspoon oregano and serve with Baked Ratatouille (page 62).

Make It Even Faster: Cook the cauliflower in your Instant Pot® or pressure cooker. Pour ½ cup water in the pot and insert a steamer basket. Turn the pot to Sauté (or heat a pressure cooker over medium-high heat). Prepare the cauliflower florets and add them to the basket. Turn off the Sauté function. Lock the lid and program for 3 minutes at low pressure. Use a quick release. Transfer the cooked cauliflower to a bowl (or pour the water out and return to the pot), add the milk, and mash as directed.

Soy-free option: Use a soy-free milk.

Per serving: Calories: 58; Total fat: 1g; Total carbs: 11g; Fiber: 5g; Sugar: 5g; Protein: 4g; Sodium: 667mg

TAHINI ROASTED VEGETABLES

GLUTEN-FREE, NUT-FREE, SOY-FREE

Serves 4 / Prep time: 10 minutes / Cook time: 15 minutes

Roasting vegetables should become a staple in your cooking repertoire. It's simple and it's a great way to use vegetables that would otherwise have been thrown away. Also, roasting brings savory meatiness to any recipe.

2 red onions, peeled and halved

1 bunch broccolini, trimmed

1 pound green beans, trimmed

2 large bell peppers (any color), seeded and cut into strips

1 tablespoon olive oil

½ teaspoon salt

¼ cup tahini

2 tablespoons lemon juice

2 teaspoons minced garlic (2 cloves)

1. Preheat the oven to 425°F. Line a large baking sheet with parchment paper.

2. In a large bowl, combine the onions, broccolini, green beans, bell pepper strips, olive oil, and salt. Toss to coat. Transfer to the lined baking sheet. Place in the oven and bake until the broccolini is fork tender (softened but still crisp), about 15 minutes.

3. While the vegetables are roasting, in a small bowl place the tahini, lemon juice, and garlic. Stir to combine (you can also purée in a blender until creamy).

4. Remove the vegetables from the oven and transfer to a large bowl. Pour the tahini sauce over the vegetables, toss gently to coat, and serve.

Substitution Tip: Use ½ cup of the Peanut Sauce on page 130 to replace the tahini sauce.

Per serving: Calories: 234; Total fat: 12g; Total carbs: 28g; Fiber: 8g; Sugar: 9g; Protein: 9g; Sodium: 345mg

BARBECUE TOFU

GLUTEN-FREE OPTION, NUT-FREE, OIL-FREE OPTION

Serves 4 / Prep time: 5 minutes / Cook time: 25 minutes

You want fast? I'll give you fast *and* only three ingredients. It seems simple (it is) and it's one of those recipes that always delivers. Annie's Naturals, Brandless, and Simple Truth all make some pretty wholesome bottled sauces, and you'll be surprised by how many others at your local grocery store are also vegan. Just read the label and keep an eye out for honey and Worcestershire sauce (which contains anchovies, unless the label specifically states that it's vegan) in the ingredients to make sure what you are getting is plant-based.

---

1 (14-ounce) package extra-firm tofu, pressed and drained (see page 23)

2 teaspoons garlic powder, divided

¾ cup jarred or bottled vegan barbecue sauce, divided

1. Preheat the oven to 400°F. Line a small baking sheet with parchment paper.

2. Cut the tofu into 4 "steaks" by slicing the block of tofu in half crosswise and then cutting each half lengthwise. Place the tofu steaks on the lined baking sheet.

3. Sprinkle 1 teaspoon of the garlic powder over the tofu steaks. Drizzle ¼ cup of the barbecue sauce over the tofu steaks. Flip each piece over and repeat with the remaining garlic powder and another ¼ cup of barbecue sauce.

4. Bake for 25 minutes. At 12 minutes, flip the tofu over and drizzle the remaining ¼ cup barbecue sauce over it and continue to bake until done.

Substitution Tip: If you prefer a homemade sauce, use the teriyaki sauce on page 79.

Make It Ahead: This can be prepared up to 5 days in advance; refrigerate covered tightly with plastic wrap.

Oil-free option: Use an oil-free barbecue sauce.

Gluten-free option: Use a gluten-free barbecue sauce.

Per serving: Calories: 144; Total fat: 4g; Total carbs: 20g; Fiber: 1g; Sugar: 13g; Protein: 8g; Sodium: 537mg

MUSHROOM SLOPPY JOE SANDWICH

GLUTEN-FREE OPTION, NUT-FREE, OIL-FREE OPTION

Serves 6 / Prep time: 10 minutes / Cook time: 15 minutes

I loved, loved, loved Sloppy Joe day at school. No doubt it was simply made with ground meat and a canned sauce. Here is my favorite vegan version, starring mushrooms and TVP (or TSP; see the Ingredient Tip below). I love it on a bun or toasted bread with pickles, onion, and mustard. Use whatever condiment you love, or don't garnish it at all.

½ cup dried TVP or TSP

½ cup warm water

1 teaspoon olive oil

2 teaspoons minced garlic (2 cloves)

2 large portobello mushrooms, stemmed and cut into ½-inch cubes *smaller cut*

1 small green bell pepper, seeded and diced

¾ cup marinara sauce (jarred or Marinara Sauce, page 129)

1 teaspoon chili powder

½ teaspoon salt

½ teaspoon ground cumin

½ teaspoon chipotle powder

6 vegan whole-grain buns or toasted bread

1. Combine the TVP and warm water in a small bowl. Set aside for 10 minutes to rehydrate.

2. In a large skillet over medium-high heat, heat the olive oil. Add the garlic, rehydrated TVP, mushrooms, and green bell pepper. Sauté until the green pepper is tender, about 3 minutes. Add the marinara sauce, chili powder, salt, cumin, and chipotle powder. Cook until the sauce begins to bubble. Reduce the heat to low and cook, uncovered, until nicely thickened, about 10 minutes, stirring occasionally.

3. Serve on buns or bread with your favorite condiments.

Ingredient Tip: Is TVP (textured vegetable protein, also sold as TSP or textured soy protein) new to you? It's one of my favorite pantry staples because it's dried and stores beautifully in an airtight jar in the pantry or freezer. It's a meat substitute that's low in fat and high in protein. To use it, you simply rehydrate it with an equal amount of warm water or broth. It will make an appearance later in the Lentil Loaf Squares (page 78).

Substitution Tip: If you prefer a completely mushroom-based sandwich, omit the TVP and use 3 portobello caps instead of 2.

Oil-free option: Use 1 tablespoon water instead of the oil to sauté.

Gluten-free option: Use gluten-free buns.

Per serving: Calories: 267; Total fat: 4g; Total carbs: 42g; Fiber: 7g; Sugar: 9g; Protein: 16g; Sodium: 719mg

FALAFEL-STYLE BURGERS

GLUTEN-FREE, NUT-FREE, SOY-FREE

Serves 4 / Prep time: 10 minutes / Cook time: 10 minutes

Ah, falafel. We love it at restaurants but we curse it when we try to make it at home. It either comes out too dry, crumbles at the touch, or takes way too long. The addition of flaxseed (for binding) and the decision to flatten these babies out instead of rolling them into balls help us avoid that disappointment while doing things fast and easy. This is *excellent* topped with Tzatziki (page 128) and set on a bed of leafy raw or steamed greens or in a sliced pita with spinach or arugula.

1 (15-ounce) can chickpeas, drained (but not rinsed)

2 tablespoons ground flaxseed

2 tablespoons sesame seeds

2 tablespoons chickpea flour

2 tablespoons nutritional yeast

1 tablespoon lemon juice

1 teaspoon salt

½ teaspoon ground cumin

½ teaspoon turmeric

½ teaspoon curry powder

1 to 2 tablespoons olive oil (or nonstick vegetable oil spray)

1. In a food processor, place the chickpeas, ground flaxseed, sesame seeds, chickpea flour, nutritional yeast, lemon juice, salt, cumin, turmeric, and curry powder. Pulse until completely combined, with a chunky, dough-like texture. Form into 4 patties about ½ inch thick. Set aside.

2. Heat a large, heavy skillet (cast iron is great) over medium-high heat. Add 1 tablespoon of the olive oil (or spray the pan) and heat until a droplet of water sizzles when dropped into the oil. Place the patties in the skillet and cook until golden brown on the bottom, about 5 minutes. Flip and cook until browned on the other side, another 5 minutes. Add additional olive oil, if needed, to avoid sticking.

Ingredient Tips:

- Chickpea flour (*besan*) is a staple in my pantry. It's a great gluten-free way to thicken foods, and it adds protein (21 grams in 1 cup). I use it when coating air-fried foods, as a thickener for sauces and gravies, and when making homemade pasta.
- Note that throughout the book, there are times when I specifically ask you not to rinse chickpeas. The brine from cooked chickpeas is called aquafaba. It's thick and is often used as an egg white replacement in vegan recipes. Retaining some of that liquid (by not rinsing) helps keep the falafel mixture together.

Per serving: Calories: 254; Total fat: 10g; Total carbs: 30g; Fiber: 10g; Sugar: 4g; Protein: 14g; Sodium: 594mg

JACKFRUIT PHILLY CHEESESTEAK BOWL

GLUTEN-FREE, NUT-FREE, OIL-FREE OPTION, SOY-FREE OPTION

Serves 4 / Prep time: 10 minutes / Cook time: 15 minutes

Alert: An umami bomb is about to land on your dinner table. Even without steak or bread, you won't miss a thing with this vegan take on the Philadelphia culinary treasure. Mushrooms, jackfruit, peppers, and a little homemade queso bring the texture and flavor you're looking for. Serve over brown rice or the Mashed (Riced) Cauliflower (page 48). Of course, you can always go old school and stuff it into a vegan hoagie roll.

1 tablespoon olive oil

1 large green bell pepper, seeded and cut into strips

1 large red bell pepper, seeded and cut into strips

1 small yellow or sweet onion, cut into half-moon slices (see page 6)

2 cups sliced mushrooms (portobello, baby bella, or white button)

1 (14-ounce) can or package jackfruit (if canned, rinse and drain)

1 teaspoon salt

½ teaspoon black pepper

3 slices vegan provolone cheese or 1 cup Mmm Mmm Umami Queso (page 126)

1. In a large skillet, heat the olive oil over medium-high heat. Add the peppers, onion, and mushrooms and sauté until the onions soften, about 3 minutes. Stir in the jackfruit, salt, and pepper and cook, stirring frequently, for another 5 minutes. Use a fork, if necessary, to pull the jackfruit apart while stirring to create shredded pieces.

2. *If using vegan provolone:* Place the cheese slices on top of the jackfruit and veggies. Cover, reduce the heat to medium-low, and cook until the cheese begins to look melty, about 3 minutes. *If using Mmm Mmm Umami Queso:* Pour the queso over the jackfruit and veggies. Cover, reduce the heat to medium-low, and cook for 3 minutes.

3. To serve, do not stir the cheese into the mix. Simply spoon from the skillet directly into bowls.

Ingredient Tip: Jackfruit is the latest natural vegan "meat" to hit the culinary scene. Once only found in Asian and Caribbean markets, jackfruit is now available in most grocery stores. Choose brands such as Edward and Sons, Native Forest, and Upton's Naturals. Why is it so popular? It shreds when cooked, just like a shredded meat, and is a stand-in for vegan versions of pulled pork, crab cakes, and more.

Soy-free option: Use soy-free cheese.

Oil-free option: Use ¼ cup water instead of the oil to sauté.

Per serving: Calories: 211; Total fat: 8g; Total carbs: 35g; Fiber: 4g; Sugar: 4g; Protein: 4g; Sodium: 654mg

BLACK BEAN AND SWEET POTATO TACOS

GLUTEN-FREE, NUT-FREE, OIL-FREE OPTION, SOY-FREE

Serves 4 / Prep time: 10 minutes / Cook time: 13 minutes

Why, oh why, are black beans and sweet potatoes so darn great together? Maybe it's because their combined nutrients deliver beta carotene, fiber, antioxidants, and loads of protein. Maybe because the combined flavors result in a slightly sweet savory dish. Whatever the reason, note that because both are so simply cooked and so tasty with little to no seasoning, I am light-handed with anything extra in this recipe, allowing the food to sing.

1 tablespoon olive oil

2 teaspoons minced garlic (2 cloves)

1 pound sweet potatoes, left unpeeled, cut into ½-inch cubes

1 small jalapeño pepper, thinly sliced

1 (15-ounce) can black beans, drained and rinsed

½ teaspoon salt

¼ teaspoon black pepper

8 vegan corn tortillas

Pumpkin seeds and/or pomegranate seeds for garnish (optional)

1. In a large skillet, heat the olive oil and garlic over medium-high heat together until the garlic is fragrant. Add the sweet potatoes and jalapeño and cook, stirring frequently to avoid sticking, until the sweet potatoes are tender, about 10 minutes. Add the beans, salt, and pepper, and gently stir together. Cover, reduce the heat to medium, and cook just enough to heat the black beans thoroughly, about 3 minutes.

2. Scoop the potatoes and beans into the tortillas, sprinkle with pumpkin and/or pomegranate seeds (if using), and serve.

Ingredient Tip: This is delicious as is, but feel free to add your favorite vegan toppings, chopped veggies such as onion and lettuce, and vegan sour cream.

Oil-free option: Use ¼ cup water or vegetable broth instead of the oil to sauté.

Per serving: Calories: 321; Total fat: 2g; Total carbs: 65g; Fiber: 14g; Sugar: 5g; Protein: 12g; Sodium: 394mg

LENTIL VEGGIE FLAUTAS

GLUTEN-FREE OPTION, NUT-FREE, OIL-FREE OPTION, SOY-FREE OPTION

Serves 4 / Prep time: 5 minutes / Cook time: 20 minutes

Lots of people know about taquitos: meat and cheese rolled up in corn tortillas and fried. Flautas are basically the same, except with flour tortillas. A healthier way to prepare flautas is to bake them till crispy and use a whole-grain tortilla.

Nonstick vegetable oil spray (optional)

1 teaspoon olive oil (or 1 tablespoon water)

½ cup diced onion (yellow or white)

½ cup diced carrot

1 (15-ounce) can lentils, drained and rinsed (1½ cups)

½ cup fresh or jarred salsa

2 cups loosely packed spinach

½ teaspoon salt

4 (10- or 12-inch) vegan flour, whole-grain, wheat, or gluten-free tortillas

1 cup shredded vegan cheese (optional)

¼ cup vegan sour cream (or Simple Vegan Sour Cream, page 124) (optional)

1. Preheat the oven to 400°F. Coat a medium baking sheet with non-stick vegetable oil spray, or line a baking sheet with parchment paper.

2. In a large skillet, heat the olive oil over medium-high heat. Add the onion and carrot and sauté until the onion softens, about 3 minutes. Stir in the lentils, salsa, spinach, and salt until well combined. Cover, reduce the heat to medium, and cook until the spinach has lightly wilted, about 2 minutes.

3. Spray the tortillas with nonstick vegetable oil spray on both sides and place on a large cutting board. Scoop just over 1 cup of the lentil mix into the middle of each tortilla. Roll them up tightly and place on the baking sheet, seam-side down. Bake until golden brown, about 15 minutes.

4. Serve by garnishing each flauta with ¼ cup shredded vegan cheese and 1 tablespoon vegan sour cream, if using.

Substitution Tip: Use black refried beans in place of the canned lentils.

Gluten-free option: Use vegan gluten-free tortillas.

Soy-free option: Use soy-free vegan sour cream and cheese.

Oil-free option: Use parchment paper to bake and don't spray the tortillas (though you may not get a fully crispy result) and 1 tablespoon water instead of the oil to sauté.

Per serving: Calories: 257; Total fat: 6g; Total carbs: 42g; Fiber: 12g; Sugar: 6g; Protein: 13g; Sodium: 540mg

JACKED-UP HEARTS OF PALM FRITTERS

GLUTEN-FREE OPTION, NUT-FREE, OIL-FREE OPTION, SOY-FREE

Makes 8 patties / Prep time: 15 minutes / Cook time: 10 minutes

Jackfruit and hearts of palm are two of my secret plant-based ingredients for creating a meaty texture in vegan cooking. They both flake up, making them ideal in dishes that traditionally use pork or seafood. The combo in this recipe creates a complex texture that grips the spices. I love serving these over a dinner salad or with grilled vegetables.

1 (14-ounce) can hearts of palm, drained and patted dry

1 (14-ounce) can jackfruit, rinsed and drained

½ cup panko or dried bread crumbs

¼ cup finely diced onion

¼ cup hummus (prepared or homemade; see page 33)

1 tablespoon minced garlic (3 cloves)

1 teaspoon potato starch or cornstarch

1 teaspoon salt

1 teaspoon paprika (sweet or smoked)

½ teaspoon cayenne pepper

½ teaspoon ground cumin

¼ teaspoon black pepper

1 to 2 tablespoons olive oil

1. Roughly chop the hearts of palm and pull the jackfruit into shreds with a fork. Transfer both to a large bowl. Add the panko, onion, hummus, garlic, starch, salt, paprika, cayenne, cumin, and black pepper. Combine well.

2. Scoop out ½ cup of the mixture and form into a patty. Repeat to make 8 patties.

3. Heat 1 tablespoon of the olive oil in a large skillet over medium-high heat until hot, about 2 minutes. Place the patties in the skillet and cook until golden brown, about 4 minutes per side.

Make It Ahead: The patties can be prepared a couple of days in advance and refrigerated. Plop them cold into the skillet and they will fry up beautifully.

Oil-free option: Use a griddle or air fryer to cook these up without oil, and use oil-free hummus.

Gluten-free option: Use gluten-free bread crumbs.

Per serving (1 fritter): Calories: 120; Total fat: 3g; Total carbs: 21g; Fiber: 3g; Sugar: 1g; Protein: 4g; Sodium: 538mg

CASHEW TEMPEH STIR-FRY

GLUTEN-FREE OPTION

Serves 4 / Prep time: 15 minutes / Cook time: 15 minutes

The key to a fast stir-fry is to start with bold flavors and use quick-cooking vegetables. Serve it over brown rice or with steamed potatoes—both perfect foils for the zing of flavor.

1 (8-ounce) package tempeh, cut into 16 cubes

1 cup raw cashews, divided

1 tablespoon minced garlic (3 cloves)

1 tablespoon unseasoned rice vinegar

1 tablespoon soy sauce or tamari

1 teaspoon ground cinnamon

1 teaspoon ground turmeric

1 teaspoon ground cumin

1 teaspoon chili powder

2 to 4 tablespoons water

2 large carrots

1 large red bell pepper

1 large yellow bell pepper

6 ounces kale

1 tablespoon vegetable oil

1. In a medium bowl, place the cubed tempeh.

2. Into a blender or food processor, place ¾ cup of the cashews, the garlic, vinegar, soy sauce, cinnamon, turmeric, cumin, and chili powder. Pulse, adding water as needed to achieve a texture slightly thinner than peanut sauce. Pour over the tempeh. Set aside.

3. Dice the carrots, seed and slice the red and yellow peppers into strips, and de-stem and chop the kale. Finely chop the remaining ¼ cup cashews.

4. In a large skillet or wok over medium heat, heat the oil. Drain the tempeh, reserving the sauce. Add the tempeh to the skillet and stir-fry until it begins to brown, 4 to 6 minutes. Add the vegetables and stir-fry until the kale has brightened and the carrots are tender, 3 to 5 minutes.

5. Pour in the reserved sauce and cashews, stir to combine, and serve.

Gluten-free option: Use gluten-free soy sauce or tamari and gluten-free tempeh.

Per serving: Calories: 416; Total fat: 26g; Total carbs: 29g; Fiber: 5g; Sugar: 4g; Protein: 20g; Sodium: 306mg

THE ART OF PERFECT TEMPEH

Many people—including me—prefer to steam tempeh before using it in a recipe. But the name of the game here is 30 minutes or less, right? If you prefer a tender, less dense tempeh texture, use the sauce ingredients as a marinade. Cube the tempeh, place it in a shallow dish with a lid or into a plastic bag, and pour the marinade over it. Store in the refrigerator overnight (or up to 3 days) before using it in this recipe.

Mediterranean Buddha Bowl, page 67

4

Five Ingredients

I know this is the chapter you've been waiting for! I have taken care to choose ingredients and seasonings that combined will deliver great taste and satiety, ever so simply. I use some prepared items (bottled teriyaki sauce, for instance) to make recipes quick and easy. In both instances—flavorful whole foods and healthy prepared foods—I'm coaching you to think about how you can prepare meals using either option. Sometimes it's all about the fresh whole food, and other times we need a little healthy helper from the grocery store. It's exactly how I cook in my own kitchen. In addition to the five *main* ingredients for each recipe, the following ingredients may be called for: water, vegetable oil (or vegetable broth as an oil-free alternative), salt, and pepper.

VEGGIE SPRING ROLLS

GLUTEN-FREE OPTION, OIL-FREE OPTION, SOY-FREE OPTION

Serves 4 / Prep time: 15 minutes / Cook time: 5 minutes

This is a really fun recipe to make with kids. We get to use our hands to roll 'em up *and* to eat them! You can find rice noodles, rice wrappers, and peanut sauce in the international aisle of your local grocer, as well as at Asian markets.

3 cups water

1 (8-ounce) package thin rice noodles

1 (8-ounce) jar peanut sauce (or 1 cup Peanut Sauce, page 130)

1 large cucumber

2 small red bell peppers

8 rice wrappers (also called spring roll skins)

1. In a small saucepan, bring the water to a boil. In a large heatproof bowl, place the rice noodles and pour the hot water over them. Let sit until the noodles soften but are still firm, about 3 minutes. Drain, return the noodles to the bowl, and pour the peanut sauce over the noodles. Toss gently to coat; set aside.

2. Leaving the peel on the cucumber, cut it in half and then julienne each half to create 16 (¼-inch-wide) sticks.

3. Cut a circle around the top of each red pepper. Pull the stem out of the peppers and run under water to remove the seeds. Cut each into four parts, and then slice into 16 strips total.

4. Dip 1 rice wrapper in warm water until moistened, about 5 seconds. Place the moist rice wrapper on a work surface and let sit until pliable, about 30 seconds. Add one eighth of the noodles and sauce, 2 cucumber sticks, and 2 pepper strips. Lift one side of the rice wrapper and fold over the filling, tucking it under the filling. Fold in the sides and continue rolling until you come to the end of the wrapper. Repeat to make 7 more spring rolls.

Substitution Tip: Use whatever raw vegetables you have on hand. Carrot or zucchini sticks, fresh basil leaves, or shredded cabbage. So many possibilities!

Gluten-free option: Use a gluten-free peanut sauce.

Oil-free option: Use an oil-free peanut sauce.

Soy-free option: Use a soy-free peanut sauce.

Per serving: Calories: 551; Total fat: 14g; Total carbs: 91g; Fiber: 6g; Sugar: 25g; Protein: 13g; Sodium: 1118mg

SMOKY COLESLAW

GLUTEN-FREE, NUT-FREE, OIL-FREE, SOY-FREE OPTION

Serves 4 / Prep time: 10 minutes

As far as I'm concerned, coleslaw doesn't get the credit it deserves. Sure, we think of it as a summer side at a picnic, but I consider it a flavorful substitute for plain lettuce and a fantastic salad base. I also really love it as a garnish. This is *amazing* in Black Bean and Sweet Potato Tacos (page 54) and Simple Spicy Tostadas (page 68).

**1 pound bagged
shredded cabbage**

**½ cup unsweetened plain
vegan yogurt**

¼ cup unseasoned rice vinegar

1 tablespoon sugar

½ teaspoon smoked paprika

½ teaspoon salt

¼ teaspoon black pepper

1. Into a large bowl, place the cabbage.

2. In a medium bowl, whisk together the yogurt, vinegar, sugar, paprika, salt, and pepper. Or, combine the dressing ingredients in a blender and purée until creamy, about 15 seconds.

3. Pour the dressing over the cabbage and mix with a spoon or spatula until the cabbage shreds are coated. Cover and chill for an hour before serving.

Substitution Tip: Swap Simple Vegan Sour Cream (page 124) or vegan mayonnaise for the vegan yogurt.

Make It Ahead: This can be prepared up to 4 days in advance; refrigerate in an airtight container.

Soy-free option: Use soy-free vegan yogurt.

Per serving: Calories: 62; Total fat: 1g; Total carbs: 12g; Fiber: 3g; Sugar: 8g; Protein: 2g; Sodium: 313mg

BAKED RATATOUILLE

GLUTEN-FREE, NUT-FREE, SOY-FREE

Serves 4 / Prep time: 10 minutes / Cook time: 36 minutes

Traditionally stewed, this summer vegetable dish is lovely baked and oh so pretty. I serve it with polenta fresh out of the oven, but ratatouille is delicious cold, too. If you have any left over, store it in the fridge and serve cold over crusty bread or toss with chopped lettuce for a veggie-filled salad.

1 large zucchini

1 small eggplant

2 teaspoons olive oil, divided

1 small red onion, cut into half-moon slices (see page 6)

1 (24-ounce) jar marinara sauce (or 3 cups Marinara Sauce, page 129)

½ cup roughly chopped or torn fresh basil leaves

½ teaspoon salt

¼ teaspoon black pepper

1. Preheat the oven to 400°F.

2. Slice the zucchini and eggplant (peel on) into ¼-inch rounds. Set aside.

3. In a saucepan, heat 1 teaspoon of the olive oil over medium-high heat. Add the onion and sauté until the onion softens, about 3 minutes. Add the marinara sauce and cook until simmering, 1 to 3 minutes.

4. Reserve ¾ cup of the sauce and transfer the rest of it to an 8-inch square baking pan with 2-inch sides. Arrange the basil over the sauce. Place the zucchini and eggplant rounds over the basil and sauce. Drizzle the remaining 1 teaspoon olive oil over the vegetables and sprinkle with the salt and pepper. Pour the reserved ¾ cup sauce over everything.

5. Cover the pan with aluminum foil and bake for 20 minutes. Remove the foil and bake until the zucchini is tender, about another 10 minutes.

Make It Ahead: Prepare the Marinara Sauce in advance, and you'll be ready to make a fully homemade meal quickly.

Per serving: Calories: 123; Total fat: 3g; Total carbs: 25g; Fiber: 8g; Sugar: 14g; Protein: 5g; Sodium: 354mg

TASTY TABOULI

NUT-FREE, OIL-FREE OPTION, SOY-FREE

Serves 4 / Prep time: 30 minutes

This traditional Lebanese dish is fantastic in lettuce-leaf boats, tossed in a kale salad, scooped into pita bread, or as a side dish (try it with the Chana Masala, page 74). No cooking required; I think you're going to like the fresh result.

¼ cup bulgur wheat

2 cups boiling water

2 large lemons, juiced

2 cups tightly packed chopped flat-leaf parsley leaves (about 3 bunches)

8 ounces cherry or grape tomatoes, halved and then quartered

1 cup finely chopped scallions (about 1 bunch), white and green parts

1 teaspoon salt

½ teaspoon black pepper

1 teaspoon olive oil (optional)

1. Into a large bowl, place the bulgur, pour the boiling water over it, cover, and let soak for 20 minutes.

2. Drain the bulgur to remove any excess water and return to the bowl. Add the lemon juice, parsley, tomatoes, scallions, salt, and pepper. Toss gently. Drizzle the olive oil (if using) over the salad and gently toss again.

3. If serving for a meal, allow it to sit for an hour or so on the counter to let the bulgur absorb the flavors.

Ingredient Tip: Bulgur wheat is so quick cooking—a simple soak is all you need. Double the bulgur in this recipe and save half to use in a salad or as a breakfast grain later in the week.

Make It Ahead: This can be prepared up to 5 days in advance; refrigerate in an airtight container.

Oil-free option: Omit the olive oil.

Per serving: Calories: 68; Total fat: 1g; Total carbs: 16g; Fiber: 5g; Sugar: 3g; Protein: 3g; Sodium: 607mg

SKILLET SEITAN STEW

GLUTEN-FREE OPTION, NUT-FREE, OIL-FREE OPTION, SOY-FREE

Serves 4 / Prep time: 5 minutes / Cook time: 15 minutes

Centuries old, seitan was the vegan meat of choice for Chinese monks. A great source of protein, this "wheat meat" delivers spot-on texture for recreating meaty dishes. This recipe is wholesome, comforting, and cooks up in one skillet with very few ingredients.

1 (8-ounce) package cubed seitan or Simple Steamed Seitan (page 131), cut into 1-inch cubes

1 tablespoon olive oil (or ¼ cup water or vegetable broth)

1 large carrot, diced (don't peel)

1 cup sliced mushrooms (baby bellas, white button, or your favorite mushroom)

1 (14.5-ounce) can seasoned diced tomatoes (Italian or with basil, garlic, and oregano)

1½ cups beef-style vegan broth or vegetable broth

½ teaspoon salt

¼ teaspoon black pepper

1. In a large skillet, heat the seitan and olive oil together over medium-high heat until the seitan begins to brown, about 5 minutes. Add the carrot, mushrooms, tomatoes, broth, salt, and pepper and bring to a boil.

2. Cover, reduce the heat to medium low, and simmer until the carrots are tender, about 10 minutes.

Gluten-free option: Use 2 cups soy curls (learn more about them on page 25), an 8-ounce package of tempeh, or a 10-ounce package of frozen gluten-free beefless tips (such as Gardein or Simple Truth).

Oil-free option: Instead of browning in the oil, simmer the seitan in ¼ cup water or vegetable broth until it evaporates.

Per serving: Calories: 297; Total fat: 7g; Total carbs: 9g; Fiber: 4g; Sugar: 4g; Protein: 45g; Sodium: 1321mg

TWO-ALARM CHILI

GLUTEN-FREE, NUT-FREE, OIL-FREE OPTION, SOY-FREE

Serves 2 / Prep time: 5 minutes / Cook time: 15 minutes

I keep a wide variety of canned beans and tomatoes in my pantry. If all else fails, I know I can combine the two with broth and water and end up with a quick soup. But I don't just keep plain, diced tomatoes on hand. I also have seasoned tomatoes (basil, oregano, and garlic, as well as fire-roasted tomatoes) so that when I'm too busy (or lazy) to measure out spices, I've already got them in a can. One pepper + conveniently peppery tomatoes = two-alarm chili.

1 teaspoon olive oil

1 small onion, diced

2 teaspoons minced garlic (2 cloves)

1 (15-ounce) can dark red kidney beans, drained and rinsed

1 heaping tablespoon minced jalapeño pepper (about 1 medium jalapeño)

1 (28-ounce) can fire-roasted tomatoes

½ cup water

1. In a large saucepan or pot over medium-high heat, cook the olive oil, onion, and garlic until the onion softens, about 3 minutes. Add the beans, jalapeño, tomatoes, and water and bring to a boil.

2. Cover, reduce the heat to medium-low, and simmer for 10 minutes.

Substitution Tip: Any bean will do.

Oil-free option: Use 1 tablespoon water instead of the oil to sauté

Per serving: Calories: 383; Total fat: 6g; Total carbs: 65g; Fiber: 20g; Sugar: 14g; Protein: 20g; Sodium: 765mg

BASIC BUDDHA BURRITO BOWL

GLUTEN-FREE, NUT-FREE, OIL-FREE OPTION, SOY-FREE OPTION

Serves 4 / Prep time: 15 minutes / Cook time: 20 minutes

Buddha bowls, also known as "hippie" bowls, used to be a way to sort of poke fun at vegan eating: "All you eat is beans, greens, and grains!" But, hey, what's wrong with that? There are so many choices! And, for the lazy (or just plain tired) cook, it simply means assembling the plant-based elements—a cooked grain, vegetables (raw, cooked, or both), protein, sauce or dressing, and a colorful garnish such as nuts or seeds—all together in one bowl. This bowl is burrito-style, just one of so many ways you can create a bowl based on your favorite flavor profiles (see sidebar for a few ideas).

1 cup quinoa

2 cups water

½ teaspoon salt (optional)

2 teaspoons olive oil

1 (15-ounce) can black beans, drained and rinsed

16 ounces (about 8 cups) fresh spinach, trimmed and chopped

½ cup salsa (fresh or jarred)

¼ cup vegan sour cream (or Simple Vegan Sour Cream, page 124)

1. In a medium saucepan, combine the quinoa, water, and salt (if using), and bring to a boil over medium-high heat. Once boiling, cover, reduce the heat to medium-low, and simmer until the water is absorbed and the quinoa is tender, 15 to 20 minutes. Remove from the heat and set aside, still covered, for 5 minutes before fluffing with a fork.

2. While the quinoa cooks, in a large skillet over medium-high heat, heat the oil for 1 minute. Add the beans and spinach and toss gently until the spinach turns dark green and begins to wilt, 3 to 4 minutes.

3. To serve, portion the quinoa into four bowls, then portion out the sautéed beans and spinach. Top each bowl with 2 tablespoons salsa and 1 tablespoon sour cream.

Make It Ahead: Batch cooking is your best friend for Buddha bowls. Any legume partnered with vegetables and grains (or starches, like sweet potatoes or parsnips) qualifies. That's why every weekend I prepare a batch of beans and a batch of grains or starch vegetables; during the week I can reheat and quickly assemble a tasty bowl with a steamed, roasted, or sautéed veggie and a little sauce or dressing.

Oil-free option: Use 1 tablespoon vegetable broth instead of the oil and use Simple Vegan Sour Cream or omit.

Soy-free option: Use a soy-free vegan sour cream.

Per serving: Calories: 355; Total fat: 9g; Total carbs: 54g; Fiber: 14g; Sugar: 2g; Protein: 19g; Sodium: 304mg

THREE FLAVOR-BOMB BOWLS

Indian: Basmati rice, red lentils, steamed broccoli, and cashew sauce with curry powder

Chinese: Brown rice, cubed baked tofu, roasted cauliflower, and soy sauce

Mediterranean: Pearled barley, gigante or other white beans, halved cherry tomatoes, and sliced green olives, garnished with fresh oregano and served with a drizzle of fresh lemon juice

SIMPLE SPICY TOSTADAS

GLUTEN-FREE OPTION, NUT-FREE, SOY-FREE OPTION

Serves 4 / Prep time: 10 minutes / Cook time: 10 minutes

So, you know I'm a chef, right? And I teach cooking classes for a living? Knowing this, you also need to know that this dinner is on our rotation weekly. Yep. Because *we all* want fast and easy food and this is the perfect example of doing it simply—and well.

---

8 vegan corn tortillas

Nonstick vegetable oil spray (optional)

1 (15-ounce) can vegetarian refried pinto or black beans

1 small onion, cut into half-moon slices (see page 6)

1 cup shredded vegan cheese

½ cup salsa

1. Preheat the oven to 400°F.

2. On a baking sheet, spritz tortillas with nonstick vegetable oil spray and place them oil-side down. Spread 3 tablespoons of refried beans on each tortilla. Cover each with onion slices. Sprinkle 2 tablespoons shredded vegan cheese over each.

3. Place the baking sheet in the oven and bake until the tortillas are crisp, about 10 minutes.

4. Scoop 2 tablespoons salsa on each tostada and serve.

Substitution Tip: Not an onion fan? Use chopped mushrooms.
Gluten-free option: Use a gluten-free nonstick vegetable oil spray; some contain flour.
Soy-free option: Use soy-free vegan cheese.

Per serving: Calories: 283; Total fat: 9g; Total carbs: 45g; Fiber: 9g; Sugar: 2g; Protein: 9g; Sodium: 764mg

RED "RISOTTO"

GLUTEN-FREE, NUT-FREE, OIL-FREE OPTION, SOY-FREE

Serves 4 / Prep time: 5 minutes / Cook time: 30 minutes

Buttery, creamy risotto is what most of us think of when cooking with arborio rice. But when I want to cook with lower or no added fats, I opt for tangy flavors, and that's what you'll get in this red version of risotto. Note, though, that we aren't making traditional risotto—no standing and stirring here—so we're cooking it like regular rice. Easy!

1 cup arborio rice

3 cups vegetable broth

1 cup jarred or canned marinara sauce (or Marinara Sauce, page 129)

¼ cup nutritional yeast

1 lemon, juiced

½ teaspoon salt

½ teaspoon black pepper

1. In a large saucepan, combine the rice, broth, and marinara sauce and bring to a boil. Cover with a tight-fitting lid, reduce the heat to a low simmer, and cook 20 minutes. At 15 minutes check on the rice to ensure there's plenty of liquid; add water as necessary.

2. Remove the pan from the heat. Let steam with the lid on for 10 minutes.

3. While fluffing the rice with a fork, add the nutritional yeast, lemon juice, salt, and pepper and combine well, then serve.

Make It Even Faster: Combine the rice, broth, and marinara sauce in an Instant Pot® or pressure cooker and set to cook for 7 minutes on high pressure. Use a natural release, then pick up with step 3.

Oil-free option: Use an oil-free marinara sauce.

Per serving: Calories: 268; Total fat: 2g; Total carbs: 49g; Fiber: 5g; Sugar: 4g; Protein: 16g; Sodium: 889mg

KALE PESTO PENNE

GLUTEN-FREE OPTION, OIL-FREE OPTION, SOY-FREE

Serves 4 / Prep time: 5 minutes / Cook time: 10 minutes

I've made a point to limit the amount of pasta in this cookbook, simply because I want you to learn that vegan eating goes way beyond salads and pasta. Nevertheless, healthy pasta meals are great to add to your dinner rotation and are super kid-friendly. This one tends toward the adult side of things with an earthy pesto sauce. If you think the kids will scrunch up their noses, just set aside a plain serving of pasta for them and toss it in vegan butter or in Marinara Sauce (page 129).

8 cups water

1 (8-ounce) package vegan penne pasta

3 cups tightly packed chopped kale

½ cup walnuts

¼ cup lemon juice

1 tablespoon minced garlic (3 cloves)

1 teaspoon salt

½ teaspoon black pepper

1 to 3 tablespoons olive oil

1. In a large pot, bring the water to a boil. Add the pasta and cook for 6 to 12 minutes (refer to the pasta package for the exact cooking time).

2. While the pasta cooks, put the kale, walnuts, lemon juice, garlic, salt, and pepper into a food processor. Pulse until it forms a thick, chunky sauce. If it is too thick to pour, drizzle in the olive oil, 1 tablespoon at a time, as needed.

3. Drain the pasta and transfer to a large bowl. Pour the pesto over the pasta. Toss gently to combine and serve.

Oil-free option: Substitute water for the oil.
Gluten-free option: Use gluten-free vegan pasta.

Per serving: Calories: 390; Total fat: 18g; Total carbs: 51g; Fiber: 4g; Sugar: 3g; Protein: 11g; Sodium: 607mg

CHEEZY ZUCCHINI LASAGNA

GLUTEN-FREE, NUT-FREE

Serves 4 / Prep time: 10 minutes / Cook time: 15 minutes

This low-carb version of the traditional baked Italian dish uses a vegetable noodle. While zucchini is the standard go-to, yellow squash works, too. With two small squash, you could use both and eat the rainbow.

1 large zucchini

1 teaspoon olive oil

16 ounces marinara sauce (canned, jarred, or Marinara Sauce, page 129)

2 cups vegan ricotta (or Ch-ofu Ricotta, page 125)

1 teaspoon black pepper

1. Preheat the oven to 375°F.

2. Slice the zucchini lengthwise into thin strips (about ⅛ inch thick) using a mandoline or knife.

3. Spread the oil over the bottom of an 8-inch square baking pan with 2-inch sides. Line the bottom of the pan with zucchini slices, overlapping them slightly, using 3 to 4 slices. Spread ½ cup of the marinara sauce over the slices. Dollop about ½ cup of vegan ricotta over the sauce. Add another layer of zucchini, ½ cup sauce, and ½ cup ricotta; repeat the layers one more time. Pour the remaining ½ cup sauce over everything and dot the top with the remaining ricotta. Sprinkle with the pepper.

4. Bake, uncovered, until the sauce is bubbling and the ricotta browns, about 15 minutes.

5. Remove from the oven and let stand for 10 minutes before serving.

Make It Ahead: The entire lasagna can be prepared up to 3 days in advance, covered, and refrigerated. It may take a bit longer to heat through.

Per serving: Calories: 168; Total fat: 4g; Total carbs: 23g; Fiber: 8g; Sugar: 6g; Protein: 16g; Sodium: 152mg

PEANUTTY CARROT NOODLES

OIL-FREE OPTION, SOY-FREE

Serves 4 / Prep time: 5 minutes / Cook time: 2 minutes

The sweet simplicity of spiralized veggies! They've certainly added a great deal of variety to my own vegetable consumption. If you don't have a spiralizer, simply julienne the carrots; they will still cook up fast and easy in the skillet.

1 teaspoon olive oil

3 large carrots, spiralized

1 small lime, juiced

½ teaspoon salt

½ cup chopped peanuts

½ cup chopped scallions (white and green parts)

1. In a large skillet over medium-high heat, heat the olive oil. Add the carrots, cover, and cook for 2 minutes. Remove from the heat, add the lime juice and salt, and toss to coat.

2. To serve, divide the noodles between serving bowls and top each with 2 tablespoons peanuts and 2 tablespoons scallions.

Substitution Tip: Instead of adding chopped peanuts, drizzle each serving with 2 tablespoons Peanut Sauce (page 130).

Add Even More Protein: Remember that peanuts are legumes and you'll get more than 7 grams of protein per 1-ounce serving. Add even more by serving this with pre-baked tofu (Wildwood or Sweet Earth) or leftover Barbecue Tofu (page 50).

Oil-free option: Use 1 tablespoon water instead of the oil to sauté.

Per serving: Calories: 142; Total fat: 10g; Total carbs: 10g; Fiber: 3g; Sugar: 4g; Protein: 5g; Sodium: 333mg

SWEET POTATO ALFREDO

GLUTEN-FREE, SOY-FREE OPTION

Serves 4 / Prep time: 5 minutes / Cook time: 15 minutes

A "good carb" noodle option, hearty sweet potatoes grip the Alfredo sauce beautifully. This is great served on its own, but also consider serving it as a side to baked tempeh or tofu, or as a base in a hippie bowl—just add some beans.

2 tablespoons vegan butter

1 teaspoon garlic powder

¼ teaspoon nutritional yeast

1 cup unsweetened soy milk

2 sweet potatoes (1 pound total), spiralized

½ teaspoon salt

½ teaspoon black pepper

1. In a large saucepan over medium-high heat, heat the vegan butter until it melts, about 1 minute. Whisk in the garlic powder and nutritional yeast until thick, about 1 minute. Slowly whisk in the soy milk. Cook until it begins to boil.

2. Add the spiralized sweet potatoes, stirring to coat them with the sauce, and bring back to a boil. Cover, reduce the heat to low, and cook until the sweet potatoes are tender, 5 to 10 minutes. Season with salt and pepper, and serve.

Substitution Tip: Any spiralized veggie will work. You just may need to adjust your cooking time accordingly. To make this recipe even faster, look for fresh or frozen spiralized carrots or squash at the grocery store.

Soy-free option: Use soy-free vegan butter and milk.

Per serving: Calories: 176; Total fat: 6g; Total carbs: 22g; Fiber: 7g; Sugar: 3g; Protein: 11g; Sodium: 404mg

CHANA MASALA

GLUTEN-FREE, NUT-FREE, OIL-FREE OPTION, SOY-FREE

Serves 6 / Prep time: 5 minutes / Cook time: 20 minutes

Chopping, simmering, and stirring are the heart of chana masala. And so is the addition of many spices. With only five main ingredients, this version boasts less chopping, fewer spices to measure, and a shorter cooking time, but it still packs a surprising and fresh boost of flavor. Serve it in a bowl like stew, or spoon it over the Mashed (Riced) Cauliflower (page 48) or a baked sweet potato.

2 teaspoons olive oil

1 medium onion, cut into slices

1 small jalapeño or serrano pepper, seeded and minced

2 teaspoons garam masala

1 teaspoon salt

1 teaspoon black pepper

1 (14.5-ounce) can roasted-garlic diced tomatoes or plain diced tomatoes

2 (15-ounce) cans chickpeas, drained but not rinsed, divided

1 to 4 tablespoons water

1. In a large saucepan, heat the olive oil over medium-high heat until a splash of water sizzles, 1 to 2 minutes. Add the onion and minced pepper and sauté until the onion softens, about 3 minutes. Add the garam masala, salt, and pepper and sauté for 2 minutes more. Stir in the tomatoes and ½ cup of the chickpeas.

2. Use an immersion blender to roughly purée the mixture in the pan. You're looking for a thick, chunky salsa-like texture. Alternatively, use a potato masher to mash the mixture in the pot.

3. Add the remainder of the chickpeas and bring to a boil. Reduce the heat to low and simmer for 10 minutes, stirring occasionally. Add water, if necessary, to maintain a thick, stew-like consistency.

Substitution Tip: A multitude of spices is the typical star of traditional chana masala, and that's why I opted for garam masala, a single spice blend that can bring lots of flavor into a five-ingredient dish. If you don't have it on hand, a one-ingredient swap is curry powder. If you're willing to go with two spices, opt for 1 teaspoon each of ground allspice and cumin.

Oil-free option: Use 2 tablespoons water instead of the oil to sauté.

Per serving: Calories: 210; Total fat: 4g; Total carbs: 34g; Fiber: 10g; Sugar: 7g; Protein: 10g; Sodium: 481mg

DELECTABLE DAL

GLUTEN-FREE, NUT-FREE, OIL-FREE OPTION, SOY-FREE

Serves 4 / Prep time: 5 minutes / Cook time: 20 minutes

I'm pretty sure I have a variation of red lentils in every single cookbook I've written. This fast-cooking lentil—much like a split pea—is packed with protein, and because it gets creamy when cooked, it's perfect as a bean dip or a surprising side (so good with the Tahini Roasted Vegetables on page 49).

1 teaspoon olive oil

1 cup chopped carrot

2 teaspoons minced garlic
(2 cloves)

1 teaspoon fennel seeds,
crushed in a mortar and pestle

1 cup dried red lentils

2 ¼ cups water

2 tablespoons lemon juice
(about 1 small lemon)

1 teaspoon salt

1. In a large saucepan over medium-high heat, heat the olive oil. Add the carrot and garlic and sauté for 3 minutes, stirring frequently to keep the garlic from sticking. Add the fennel seeds, lentils, and water.

2. Bring to a boil, cover, reduce the heat to medium-low or low, and simmer until the lentils are tender, 15 to 20 minutes.

3. Remove from the heat, stir in the lemon juice and salt, mash and stir until thick and creamy, and serve.

Make It Even Faster: Break out the Instant Pot® or pressure cooker! Red lentils cook up very fast. Follow step 1 in an uncovered pressure cooker or multicooker pot using the Sauté function. In step 2, lock the lid and cook at high pressure for 5 minutes. Use a natural release and finish as directed in step 3.

Oil-free option: Use 2 teaspoons water instead of the oil to sauté.

Per serving: Calories: 196; Total fat: 2g; Total carbs: 32g; Fiber: 16g; Sugar: 3g; Protein: 13g; Sodium: 605mg

GREEN CHILE BLACK BEAN BURGERS

GLUTEN-FREE OPTION, NUT-FREE, OIL-FREE, SOY-FREE

Serves 4 / Prep time: 15 minutes / Cook time: 12 minutes

I feel morally obligated to include a veggie burger recipe in this book. And I feel equally obligated to make it simple with a good ol' punch of flavor, so I'm using canned green chiles. They not only kick up the taste, they also provide just the right amount of liquid to hold the patties together. Serve these burgers on buns or lettuce wraps—or crumbled in tacos—with a healthy dose of your favorite hot sauce.

---

1 (15-ounce) can black beans, drained and rinsed

½ cup rolled oats

2 tablespoons ground flaxseed

1 (4-ounce) can green chiles, undrained

1 teaspoon garlic powder

1. Preheat the oven to 400°F. Line a baking sheet with parchment paper.

2. In a medium bowl, mash the beans with a fork or potato masher. Add the rolled oats, ground flaxseed, green chiles, and garlic powder. Combine well with a wooden spoon or using your hands. Form 4 patties ¾ inch thick and place on the baking sheet.

3. Bake for 6 minutes. Flip over and bake until the burgers are lightly browned and crisp, about 6 more minutes.

Substitution Tip: Use pinto, kidney, or cannellini beans instead of black beans.

Gluten-free option: Use certified gluten-free oats.

Per serving: Calories: 183; Total fat: 2g; Total carbs: 31g; Fiber: 10g; Sugar: 2g; Protein: 10g; Sodium: 116mg

PITA PIZZA, TOO

GLUTEN-FREE OPTION, NUT-FREE, OIL-FREE OPTION, SOY-FREE

Serves 4 / Prep time: 15 minutes / Cook time: 8 minutes

We started with a fast, uncooked Salad Pita Pizza (page 35) in chapter 2, and now we're going to build texture and flavor with an equally easy baked version. Still using a bean base—for protein and a creamy alternative to cheese—just a little sweet onion delivers big on flavor. Delicious as is, this pizza is also tasty with any of your favorite veggies to bring color and additional nutrients. Mushrooms, baby spinach, and sliced bell peppers are my favorite add-ons.

1 large bell pepper (any kind)

1 tablespoon olive oil or nonstick vegetable oil spray (optional)

4 (6- or 8-inch) vegan pita breads

1 (15-ounce) can vegetarian refried pinto or black beans

½ cup tomato sauce (canned or make your own with tomato powder, page 10)

2 cups sliced onion (sweet or Vidalia)

Salt

Black pepper

1. Preheat the oven to 400°F. Line a baking sheet with parchment paper.

2. Slice the bell pepper into rings: First, cut a circle around the top of the pepper. Pull the stem out of the pepper and run under water to remove seeds. Place the pepper on one side and thinly slice the pepper crosswise for 8 pepper rings. Set aside.

3. Brush olive oil on both sides of each piece of pita (or coat with nonstick vegetable oil spray).

4. Spread about ½ cup refried beans on one piece of pita bread. Spread 2 tablespoons of tomato sauce over the beans. Add ½ cup sliced onion and 2 bell pepper rings. Add a pinch of salt and a pinch of pepper. Repeat to create 4 pita pizzas.

5. Place the pitas on the prepared baking sheet and bake until the pitas turn golden brown and crispy, about 8 minutes.

Substitution Tip: Try this pizza on corn, wheat, or flour vegan tortillas.
Gluten-free option: Use gluten-free vegan pita bread.
Oil-free option: Omit the olive oil and cooking spray; the pita will be a bit less crispy.

Per serving: Calories: 342; Total fat: 7g; Total carbs: 62g; Fiber: 13g; Sugar: 6g; Protein: 13g; Sodium: 670mg

LENTIL LOAF SQUARES

GLUTEN-FREE OPTION, NUT-FREE, OIL-FREE OPTION

Serves 9 / Prep time: 25 minutes / Cook time: 25 minutes

You can find a zillion lentil loaf recipes and all have their merits. A five-ingredient version may seem aspirational, and understandably so. Most loaves use lots of ingredients to help the loaf "stand up." In this version, I opt for a different shape, which allows me to use fewer ingredients without compromising flavor. The starchy arborio and TVP bind this together beautifully. This is one of the longer-cooking recipes in this chapter but the actual work is minimal. Use the baking time to prep some food for tomorrow!

½ cup arborio rice

2 cups warm water, divided, plus more as needed

½ cup TVP (textured vegetable protein)

Nonstick vegetable oil spray

1 (15-ounce) can lentils, drained and rinsed

½ cup finely diced onion

¼ teaspoon black pepper

¾ cup teriyaki sauce, prepared or homemade (see sidebar), divided

1. In a medium saucepan, combine the rice and 1½ cups of the water and bring to a boil. Cover with a tight-fitting lid, reduce the heat to a low simmer, and cook for 20 minutes. At 15 minutes, check on the rice to ensure there's plenty of liquid; add water as necessary.

2. In a small bowl, combine the TVP and remaining ½ cup water to rehydrate the TVP while the rice cooks.

3. Preheat the oven to 400°F. Lightly grease an 8-inch square baking pan with 2-inch sides with nonstick vegetable oil spray.

4. Once the rice is cooked, transfer it to a large bowl. Add the lentils, rehydrated TVP, onion, and pepper. Combine well, using a potato masher or your hands to mash everything together. Pour ½ cup of the teriyaki sauce into the bowl and mix well with a wooden spoon or spatula.

5. Transfer the mixture to the prepared pan, smoothing it into an even thickness and pushing it into the corners. Pour the remaining ¼ cup teriyaki sauce over the top and spread it evenly, using a spoon or spatula.

6. Bake until the top layer of teriyaki has glazed and the edges are pulling away from the pan and have browned, about 25 minutes.

7. Remove from the oven and set aside to cool for 10 minutes. Slice the lentil loaf into 9 squares with a sharp, serrated knife.

Substitution Tip: These lentil squares are in my regular cooking rotation. I also make them with barbecue sauce and peanut sauce (for homemade, see page 130).

Make It Even Faster:

- Make the arborio rice in an Instant Pot® or pressure cooker. Use 1 cup water with ½ cup rice and cook on high pressure for 7 minutes; use a natural release, releasing after 10 minutes.
- Use 1½ cups ready-made brown rice.
- Make the arborio rice in advance.

Oil-free option: Use parchment paper to line the pan instead of non-stick spray.

Gluten-free option: Use a gluten-free teriyaki sauce; if making your own (see sidebar), opt for a gluten-free soy sauce or tamari. Use a gluten-free nonstick spray; many contain flour.

Per serving: Calories: 304; Total fat: 0g; Total carbs: 55g; Fiber: 10g; Sugar: 10g; Protein: 20g; Sodium: 2072mg

MAKE YOUR OWN 5-INGREDIENT TERIYAKI SAUCE

½ cup soy sauce or tamari

¼ cup water plus 1 tablespoon warm water

¼ cup agave syrup or vegan honey

2 teaspoons minced garlic (2 cloves)

¼ teaspoon ground ginger (or 1 tablespoon grated fresh ginger)

1¾ teaspoons arrowroot

In a small saucepan, combine the soy sauce, ¼ cup of the water, the agave, garlic, and ginger. Cook over medium-high heat until gently boiling, about 5 minutes. In a small bowl, with a fork, whisk together the arrowroot and remaining tablespoon warm water. Pour into the saucepan, stir well, reduce the heat to low, and simmer until slightly thickened, 3 to 5 minutes. Makes ¾ cup.

VEGAN CORNED BEEF AND CABBAGE

NUT-FREE, OIL-FREE OPTION, SOY-FREE OPTION

Serves 4 / Prep time: 10 minutes / Cook time: 20 minutes

I was on a mission to create a five-ingredient nod to the Irish on St. Patrick's Day years ago, and this came together just as I had hoped. (Meaning, my husband made it). The maple syrup and allspice are the subtle seasonings that recreate the familiar flavors.

8 small red potatoes, washed (unpeeled)

2½ teaspoons salt, divided

1 medium head green cabbage, quartered

1 (8-ounce) package cubed seitan or Simple Steamed Seitan (page 131), cut into 1-inch pieces

2 tablespoons maple syrup

2 teaspoons ground allspice

½ teaspoon black pepper

1 to 2 teaspoons olive oil

1. In large pot, cover the potatoes with water by about 2 inches. Add 2 teaspoons of the salt. Bring to a boil over medium heat and cook for 10 minutes. Add the cabbage to the pot and cook until the potatoes are tender, about another 10 minutes.

2. In a medium bowl, combine the seitan, maple syrup, allspice, pepper, and remaining ½ teaspoon salt. In a medium skillet, heat the olive oil over medium-high heat. Add the seitan and sauté for 5 minutes, stirring frequently. Reduce the heat to low and cook 5 minutes longer.

3. Carefully drain the potatoes and cabbage.

4. To serve, plate one quarter of the cabbage, 2 red potatoes, and one quarter of the seitan.

Make It Even Faster: If you have leftover mashed potatoes or Mashed (Riced) Cauliflower (page 48), opt for that instead of the red potatoes and you'll be eating in less than 15 minutes!

Soy-free option: Use a soy-free seitan.

Oil-free option: Use 2 tablespoons water instead of the oil to sauté.

Per serving: Calories: 336; Total fat: 3g; Total carbs: 61g; Fiber: 13g; Sugar: 16g; Protein: 19g; Sodium: 639mg

EASY AS SHEPHERD'S PIE

GLUTEN-FREE OPTION, NUT-FREE OPTION, OIL-FREE OPTION, SOY-FREE OPTION

Serves 4 / Prep time: 5 minutes / Cook time: 35 minutes

This is one of the top five recipes my husband requests on a weekly basis, which makes me extremely happy because it's really easy! Notice that once again I'm asking you to leave the peel on the potatoes. Of course, you're all grown up and you can do whatever you want, but for this recipe, I like how the peel keeps the pie pieces together. Besides, we're all too busy to peel veggies, aren't we?

1 pound russet potatoes, cubed (unpeeled)

Nonstick vegetable oil spray (optional)

1 teaspoon olive oil

12 ounces frozen green beans (or fresh green beans)

1 (15-ounce) can lentils, drained and rinsed (or 1½ cups cooked lentils)

2 tablespoons vegan Worcestershire sauce

¾ cup unsweetened soy or almond milk, divided

½ teaspoon coarse salt (or table salt)

¼ teaspoon black pepper

1. In a large saucepan or pot, cover the potatoes with water. Bring to a boil and let continue to boil until they are tender, 10 to 15 minutes.

2. Preheat the oven to 400°F. Spray an 8-inch square baking pan with 2-inch sides with nonstick vegetable oil spray (or use a nonstick pan).

3. In a large skillet, heat the olive oil over medium-high heat. Add the frozen green beans and cook for 1 minute. Add the lentils, Worcestershire sauce, and ½ cup of the milk, and combine well. Continue to cook until the mixture begins to boil. Cover and cook for 3 minutes longer. Transfer to the baking pan.

4. Drain the potatoes and return to the pot. Add the remaining ¼ cup milk and the salt and mash with a potato masher. Spread the mashed potatoes over the lentil mixture. Sprinkle with the pepper.

5. Bake until the lentils are bubbling, about 15 minutes.

6. Serve with additional salt and pepper to taste.

Make It Even Faster: For a faster—and lower-carb—option, use the Mashed (Riced) Cauliflower recipe (page 48) instead of potatoes. They cook up faster and are a bit lighter. Bake until the lentils are bubbling, 10 to 12 minutes.

Nut-free option: Use nut-free milk.

Soy-free option: Use soy-free milk.

Gluten-free option: Use a gluten-free nonstick spray or a nonstick pan.

Oil-free option: Use a nonstick pan and 1 tablespoon water instead of the oil to sauté.

Per serving: Calories: 246; Total fat: 3g; Total carbs: 45g; Fiber: 14g; Sugar: 4g; Protein: 13g; Sodium: 379mg

Protein Pasta
Primavera, page 90

5

One-Pot Wonders

There are so many reasons to love one-pot meals! Most of us would agree that fewer dishes to clean is always a motivator, but so is the mingling of flavors that occurs when you cook everything in one pot. And there's no need to worry about a side or a salad when everything is cooked together (though you will notice that I make some pairing suggestions throughout to protein things up a bit). As you cook through these recipes you'll likely notice that simplicity is the name of the game (with a few exceptions, like the jambalaya). This is vegan cooking, y'all.

SOCCA BREAD PIZZA

GLUTEN-FREE, NUT-FREE, SOY-FREE OPTION

Serves 2 / Prep time: 15 minutes / Cook time: 25 to 30 minutes

Popular throughout France, socca is a flatbread made with chickpea flour. It gives our pizza an added boost of protein—14 grams per serving—and makes it naturally gluten-free. Pour a glass of wine or a cup of tea while you wait for it to rest for a few minutes after baking.

1¼ cups water

1 cup garbanzo bean flour

1 tablespoon olive oil

2 teaspoons minced garlic (2 cloves)

½ teaspoon salt

1 cup diced red onion, divided

1 tablespoon chopped fresh chives

Nonstick vegetable oil spray

2 tablespoons tomato sauce

1 cup shredded vegan mozzarella cheese (optional)

1 cup sliced mushrooms (baby bella, cremini, or white)

1 teaspoon dried oregano

1 teaspoon red pepper flakes

¼ teaspoon black pepper

1. In a blender or food processor, blend the water, flour, oil, garlic, and salt for about 20 seconds to achieve a thick but pourable batter.

2. Preheat a 9-inch cast iron skillet in the oven at 450°F.

3. Once the oven is preheated, add ½ cup of the onion and the chives to the batter, and stir to mix.

4. Carefully remove the skillet from the oven and grease with nonstick vegetable oil spray. Pour the batter into the skillet and return it to the oven. Bake for 15 minutes.

5. Remove the skillet from the oven. Reduce the oven temperature to 425°F.

6. Spread the tomato sauce over the socca. Top with the vegan cheese (if using) and mushrooms. Sprinkle with the oregano, red pepper flakes, and pepper.

7. Return the skillet to the oven and bake until the cheese has melted, 7 to 9 minutes (note that not all vegan cheeses melt the same way, so also look for browning on the cheese and socca crust).

8. Remove the skillet from the oven and let the pizza rest for at least 5 minutes before slicing.

Substitution Tip: The vegan cheese is optional. I sometimes use a can of refried beans, spreading it over the pizza crust before adding tomato sauce, to build the protein content and deliver the creaminess we expect from melted cheese. If you try this—and I hope you do—consider switching up the toppings (hello, sliced jalapeño!) and spices.

Soy-free option: If using vegan cheese, opt for soy-free vegan mozzarella.

Per serving: Calories: 215; Total fat: 8g; Total carbs: 28g; Fiber: 11g; Sugar: 1g; Protein: 14g; Sodium: 667mg

POTATO AND PINTO BEAN HASH

GLUTEN-FREE, NUT-FREE, OIL-FREE OPTION, SOY-FREE

Serves 4 / Prep time: 10 minutes / Cook time: 15 minutes

Breakfast hash. Did you grow up eating it? In college I got introduced to hash in a can (don't judge) and, well, it was fine. Now I know that hash is really a way to use up what you have in your kitchen; traditionally, leftover meat—chopped—fried up with potato and spices. This version intentionally begins with seasoned potatoes, adding pinto beans in right at the end to make it a well-rounded meal in just one pan.

2 teaspoons olive oil

1 small onion, chopped

1 small red bell pepper, seeded and chopped

1 large (about 10 ounces) russet potato, unpeeled, cut into ¼-inch dice

1 teaspoon ground cumin

1 (15-ounce) can pinto beans, drained and rinsed

4 cups (about 5 ounces) baby spinach

½ teaspoon salt

¼ teaspoon black pepper

1. In a large skillet over medium-high heat, heat the olive oil. Add the onion, bell pepper, potato, and cumin and cook, stirring frequently, until the potato cubes are tender, about 10 minutes.

2. Reduce the heat to medium. Add the pinto beans, spinach, salt, and pepper to the pot, stir to combine, and cover to steam until the spinach begins to lightly wilt, about 3 minutes.

Substitution Tip: Sweet potatoes are terrific in this, too.

Oil-free option: Use 1 tablespoon water instead of the oil to sauté.

Per serving: Calories: 241; Total fat: 3g; Total carbs: 44g; Fiber: 10g; Sugar: 3g; Protein: 11g; Sodium: 322mg

QUINOA RAINBOW CHARD

GLUTEN-FREE, NUT-FREE, OIL-FREE, SOY-FREE

Serves 4 / Prep time: 5 minutes / Cook time: 20 minutes

Quinoa is one of the quickest-cooking whole grains (actually, it's a seed) and it provides all the nutrients, including protein, which we are looking for in a nutrient-dense meal. It's also a wonderful option whenever you're experiencing "bean fatigue."

1 cup uncooked quinoa

2 cups water

½ bunch (6 to 8 ounces) rainbow or Swiss chard

2 teaspoons balsamic vinegar

½ teaspoon salt

¼ teaspoon black pepper

1. In medium pot, combine the quinoa and water. Bring to a boil. Cover, reduce the heat to medium-low, and simmer until the water is absorbed, 15 to 20 minutes.

2. Chop the stems off the chard leaves. Stack and roll the leaves and slice, forming shreds.

3. Remove the quinoa from the stove. Uncover and add the shredded chard to the pot (don't stir), cover and set aside to steam for 5 minutes.

4. Remove the lid, add the vinegar, salt, and pepper, gently toss to combine well, and serve.

Ingredient Tip: When shopping for chard, take a look at the stalks. The multicolored (red, yellow, and green) are rainbow chard. Swiss and rainbow chard can be used interchangeably.

Per serving: Calories: 168; Total fat: 4g; Total carbs: 30g; Fiber: 4g; Sugar: 1g; Protein: 7g; Sodium: 314mg

WARM FAVA BEAN AND HEARTS OF PALM SALAD

GLUTEN-FREE, NUT-FREE, OIL-FREE OPTION, SOY-FREE

Serves 4 / Prep time: 10 minutes / Cook time: 10 minutes

Simply sautéing beans with a unique vegetable can get you out of a culinary rut, and I love using briny pickled vegetables to add a pop of flavor. This simple sautéed meal is inspired by one of the healthiest cuisines in the world: Mediterranean. You can also use butter beans or any other white bean and swap out the hearts of palm with artichoke hearts. Serve in a bowl with a hearty grain such as farro or pearl barley or over a bed of raw arugula, which will wilt slightly under the weight of the warm beans.

1 teaspoon olive oil

1 small onion, diced

2 teaspoons minced garlic (2 cloves)

1 (15-ounce) can fava beans, drained and rinsed

1 teaspoon dried basil

½ teaspoon ground cumin

¼ cup white wine vinegar

1 (14-ounce) can hearts of palm, drained and sliced into ¼-inch rounds

1. In a large skillet over medium-high heat, heat the olive oil. Add the onion and garlic and sauté until the onion softens, about 3 minutes. Add the fava beans, basil, cumin, and vinegar. Stir to combine well. Cover, reduce the heat to low, and simmer for 5 minutes.

2. Uncover, increase the heat to medium, and add the hearts of palm. Gently toss together and cook for 2 minutes, long enough to warm up the hearts of palm, then serve.

Ingredient Tip: Fava beans are also known as broad beans. When using canned fava beans, you can simply rinse and add to salads or quickly cook. Boasting 10 grams of protein per serving, they are a great entrée bean.

Oil-free option: Use 2 teaspoons water or vegetable broth instead of the oil to sauté.

Per serving: Calories: 155; Total fat: 2g; Total carbs: 26g; Fiber: 9g; Sugar: 1g; Protein: 10g; Sodium: 427mg

SPICY PINTO BEAN SKILLET

GLUTEN-FREE, NUT-FREE, OIL-FREE OPTION, SOY-FREE

Serves 4 / Prep time: 5 minutes / Cook time: 15 minutes

Some meals are as easy as this equation: flavor + beans = yum. You can scoop these peppery beans out of the skillet and into a bowl and be ready to roll. You can also serve them over rice or baked potatoes. Or use a potato masher for quick refried beans and serve them with tortilla chips.

1 tablespoon olive oil

½ cup diced onion

4 teaspoons minced garlic (4 cloves)

1 small jalapeño pepper, seeded and diced

1 teaspoon chili powder

½ teaspoon ground cumin

2 (15-ounce) cans pinto beans, drained and rinsed

1 (14.5-ounce) can diced tomatoes

1 cup vegetable broth

1. In a large skillet over medium-high heat, heat the olive oil. Add the onion, garlic, jalapeño, chili powder, and cumin and sauté until the onion softens, about 3 minutes.

2. Add the beans, tomatoes, and broth and combine well. Cook until the broth begins to bubble. Reduce the heat to medium-low, simmer for 10 minutes, and serve.

Substitution Tip: Cranberry and Anasazi beans are both excellent alternatives to pinto beans.

Oil-free option: Use ¼ cup water instead of the oil to sauté.

Per serving: Calories: 307; Total fat: 5g; Total carbs: 52g; Fiber: 17g; Sugar: 4g; Protein: 17g; Sodium: 115mg

SPAGHETTI SQUASH MARINARA

GLUTEN-FREE, NUT-FREE, OIL-FREE OPTION, SOY-FREE

Serves 2 / Prep time: 5 minutes / Cook time: 25 minutes

Cutting through a spaghetti squash requires some deft knife skills—it can be as tough to cut through as a pumpkin or butternut squash. So, I feel a little like MacGyver when I break into one. But it's worth it—the "noodles" inside are delightful. Many folks will bake it first, some pressure cook it, and some, like me, try to find a way to cook that squash into noodles as part of cooking the full meal. Give it a go!

1 spaghetti squash

1 (16-ounce) jar marinara (or 2 cups Marinara Sauce, page 129)

½ cup vegetable broth

1. Cut the spaghetti squash in half, at the middle, crosswise (not lengthwise). Scoop out the seeds. Set aside.

2. In a large pot over medium heat, bring the marinara sauce to a simmer. Add the broth, then place a 6x6x3-inch steam trivet over the mixture. Place both pieces of the spaghetti squash cut side down on the trivet. Cover, reduce the heat to medium-low, and cook until the squash is tender, about 20 minutes. Remove the squash from the pot. Holding each half with a folded clean dish towel, scrape the inside of the squash with a fork, releasing the strands of squash. Transfer the strands to the pot with the marinara sauce, discarding the empty squash halves. Toss gently to coat the squash strands well with sauce, then serve.

Make It Even Faster: Not in the mood to fuss with the spaghetti squash? Grab some fresh spiralized squash noodles in the produce section—or frozen spiralized squash—at your local grocery store.

Oil-free option: Use oil-free marinara sauce.

Per serving: Calories: 167; Total fat: 2g; Total carbs: 39g; Fiber: 4g; Sugar: 11g; Protein: 5g; Sodium: 124mg

PROTEIN PASTA PRIMAVERA

GLUTEN-FREE, NUT-FREE, OIL-FREE OPTION, SOY-FREE OPTION

Serves 4 / Prep time: 5 minutes / Cook time: 10 minutes

An upside of the increasing popularity of the gluten-free diet is that legume-based pasta is now readily available. Explore Cuisine, The Only Bean, Pow!, Sea Point Farms, and Thrive are a few good brands. Once a cliché, a plate of pasta with veggies is now considered a balanced and healthy meal, thanks to protein-rich pasta. (Please don't peel your veggies!)

2 teaspoons olive oil

1 large carrot, sliced or chopped

1 small zucchini, thinly sliced or chopped

1 small yellow squash, thinly sliced or chopped

1 tablespoon minced garlic (3 cloves)

1 teaspoon dried oregano

1 teaspoon salt

½ teaspoon dried basil

1 (8-ounce) package bean-based pasta

2 to 3 cups water

1 pint cherry or grape tomatoes, halved

½ teaspoon black pepper

1. In a pot or deep skillet over medium-high heat, heat the olive oil. Add the carrot, zucchini, yellow squash, and garlic and cook, stirring a few times, for 3 minutes. Add the oregano, salt, and basil and stir well.

2. Add the pasta and 2 cups of the water, stir to combine, and bring to a boil. Reduce the heat to medium and continue to cook, stirring frequently (and gently), until the pasta is al dente, 6 to 7 minutes. Add more of the water if necessary.

3. Stir in the tomatoes and pepper and serve.

Substitution Tip: For Alfredo-style pasta, substitute 2 cups plant-based milk for the water, and if additional liquid is required, use water.
Oil-free option: Use water instead of the oil to sauté.
Soy-free option: Use soy-free pasta.

Per serving: Calories: 261; Total fat: 4g; Total carbs: 51g; Fiber: 4g; Sugar: 7g; Protein: 9g; Sodium: 600mg

ONE-POT MAC

GLUTEN-FREE OPTION, NUT-FREE, OIL-FREE OPTION, SOY-FREE OPTION

Serves 4 / Prep time: 5 minutes / Cook time: 10 minutes

Wham, bam, I'm eating, ma'am! This is a less-fussy one-dish pasta in which you control the carbs, protein, and gluten (or not). And, it's that dish that you know you can set down in front of the kids and they will gobble it up. To veg it up, stir in a light leafy green, like baby spinach or arugula, or a cup or two of peas or corn (or both) before serving.

1 tablespoon vegan butter (optional)

1 (8-ounce) package vegan elbow pasta

2 cups chicken-style vegan broth or vegetable broth

¼ cup nutritional yeast

½ teaspoon salt

¼ teaspoon black pepper

1. In a large saucepan over medium-high heat, melt the vegan butter. Add the pasta and broth and bring to a boil. Cover, reduce the heat to medium-low, and cook, stirring occasionally to avoid sticking, until the pasta is tender, 7 to 9 minutes.

2. Remove the pan from the heat, stir in the nutritional yeast, salt, and pepper, and serve.

Ingredient Tips:

- For a protein-rich noodle, try quinoa pasta.
- For a more "adult-style" mac, sauté 2 teaspoons minced garlic and ½ cup diced onion in the vegan butter until the onion softens, about 3 minutes, before adding the pasta to the pot.

Gluten-free option: Use gluten-free pasta.

Soy-free option: Use soy-free vegan butter and pasta.

Oil-free option: Omit the vegan butter.

Per serving: Calories: 260; Total fat: 2g; Total carbs: 49g; Fiber: 6g; Sugar: 2g; Protein: 15g; Sodium: 296mg

RED JACKFRUIT JAMBALAYA

GLUTEN-FREE OPTION, NUT-FREE, OIL-FREE OPTION, SOY-FREE

Serves 6 / Prep time: 15 minutes / Cook time: 40 minutes

Traditional jambalaya is anything but vegan, but we're creative, right? Highly seasoned jackfruit stands in for sausage, and canned hearts of palm replace the seafood. The Cajun "Holy Trinity" of onion, celery, and green pepper provides the flavor foundation for this satisfying dish. Get ready to impress your friends with this one!

2 teaspoons olive oil

1 cup diced onion

½ cup diced celery

½ cup diced green bell pepper

1 (14-ounce) can or package plain jackfruit (if canned, rinse and drain), roughly chopped

2 teaspoons minced garlic (2 cloves)

1 teaspoon smoked paprika

1 teaspoon fennel seeds, crushed

½ to 1 teaspoon red pepper flakes

1 (14-ounce) can hearts of palm, drained and cut into 1-inch rounds

½ teaspoon salt

1 (14-ounce) can diced tomatoes

2 teaspoons vegan Worcestershire sauce

1 teaspoon dried thyme

1 teaspoon dried oregano

½ teaspoon black pepper

1½ cups long-grain white rice

3 cups chicken-style vegan broth or vegetable broth

1. In a large skillet over medium-high heat, heat the oil. Add the onion, celery, and bell pepper and sauté until the onion softens, 3 to 5 minutes. Add the jackfruit, breaking it apart as you stir it, garlic, paprika, fennel seeds, and red pepper flakes and sauté for another 3 minutes. Add the hearts of palm and salt and sauté until the jackfruit and hearts of palm are lightly browned, about 3 minutes.

2. Add the tomatoes, Worcestershire sauce, thyme, oregano, black pepper, rice, and broth. Stir well. Bring to a boil, then reduce the heat to low, cover, and cook until the liquid is absorbed and the rice is tender, 25 to 30 minutes, stirring occasionally.

Ingredient Tip: As discussed on page 56, jackfruit is a great whole-food stand-in for meat. Hearts of palm stand in for seafood; sliced or pulled apart, they can be used in no-tuna salads and not-crab cakes, and seared as vegan scallops.

Make It Even Faster: This is a snap to make in the pressure cooker. Follow the directions above in step 1, using the Sauté function. In step 2, add the seasonings, rice, and broth, decreasing the amount of broth from 3 cups to 2 cups. Stir well, then add the tomatoes and *do not stir*. Lock the lid, cook for 6 minutes on high pressure, and use natural release, releasing after 15 minutes.

Gluten-free option: Use gluten-free vegan Worcestershire sauce.

Oil-free option: Use 1 tablespoon water or vegetable broth instead of the oil to sauté.

Per serving: Calories: 292; Total fat: 3g; Total carbs: 63g; Fiber: 5g; Sugar: 3g; Protein: 7g; Sodium: 530mg

TEXAS CHILI

GLUTEN-FREE OPTION, NUT-FREE, OIL-FREE, SOY-FREE

Serves 4 / Prep time: 5 minutes / Cook time: 15 minutes

Texas chili is known for three things: no tomatoes, no beans, all beef. This vegan version is all about the vegan beef—seitan. Simply simmered in spice, it is delicious with sourdough bread or cornbread or served over polenta.

2 teaspoons olive oil (or 2 tablespoons vegetable broth or water)

2 (8-ounce) packages cubed seitan or 2 cups chopped Simple Steamed Seitan (page 131)

1 small yellow onion, cut into half-moon slices (see page 6)

4 teaspoons minced garlic (4 cloves)

2 teaspoons chili powder

1 teaspoon ground cumin

½ teaspoon salt

¼ teaspoon black pepper

2 cups water

1. In a pot or skillet over medium-high heat, heat the olive oil until it is hot and sizzles when a droplet of water hits the pan. Brown the seitan, stirring frequently, for about 5 minutes (drizzle water into the pan if the seitan begins to stick).

2. Add the onion, garlic, chili powder, cumin, salt, black pepper, and water and stir to combine. Bring to a boil. Cover, reduce the heat to medium-low, simmer for 10 minutes, and serve.

Substitution Tip: If you want beans instead of seitan, swap 1 (15-ounce) can white kidney beans, drained and rinsed, for the seitan, skipping step 1 and adding them with the rest of the ingredients.

Gluten-free option: Use 12 ounces jackfruit or beans (see tip above) instead of the seitan.

Per serving: Calories: 338; Total fat: 8g; Total carbs: 14g; Fiber: 4g; Sugar: 6g; Protein: 53g; Sodium: 865mg

Roasted Kabocha Squash with Chickpeas, page 101

6

Bake It Right: Sheet Pan & Casserole Dinners

Continuing the "one pot" theme, but this time in the oven, we'll focus on longer-cooking ingredients. While this book is all about the fast and easy approach to vegan cooking, let's face it: some amazing plant-based ingredients do take a bit longer to cook. But, with me as your guide, you'll discover ways to simplify and speed things up. If you want to double any of these recipes, opt for a larger sheet pan. Conversely, you can opt for a small sheet pan to cut a recipe in half. The sheet pan sizes in my kitchen are 9-by-13, 10-by-15, 11-by-17, and 13-by-18 inches. I consider a small pan to be 13 inches; medium is 15 inches; and the 17- or 18-inch pans are large.

TOFU-SPINACH CASSEROLE

GLUTEN-FREE, NUT-FREE, OIL-FREE OPTION

Serves 6 / Prep time: 10 minutes / Cook time: 33 minutes

In this recipe, take everything you might put in a skillet for a typical tofu scramble and bake it. This gives you the freedom to do other things (chop, slice, and dice to prepare for other recipes) and it provides texture variety, which is so important to our palate pleasure.

Nonstick vegetable oil spray

1 teaspoon olive oil

1 small yellow onion, diced

2 carrots, diced

1 celery stalk, diced

1 tablespoon minced garlic (3 cloves)

½ teaspoon salt

¼ teaspoon black pepper

16 ounces (about 8 cups loosely packed) baby spinach

1 (14-ounce) package extra-firm tofu, pressed and drained

¼ cup unsweetened plant-based milk

1. Preheat the oven to 375°F. Lightly coat a 9-inch square baking dish with nonstick vegetable oil spray.

2. In a large cast iron skillet or Dutch oven, heat the oil over medium-high heat. Add the onion, carrots, celery, garlic, salt, and pepper and sauté until the vegetables soften, about 3 minutes. Add the spinach, combine well, and transfer to the prepared baking pan.

3. In a food processor or blender, purée the tofu and milk together until smooth. Pour over the cooked vegetables and stir together. Bake until it's bubbling around the edges, about 30 minutes.

Substitution Tip: Try kale or Swiss chard instead of spinach.

Oil-free option: Use a nonstick baking dish instead of nonstick spray and use water instead of the oil to sauté.

Per serving: Calories: 104; Total fat: 5g; Total carbs: 8g; Fiber: 3g; Sugar: 2g; Protein: 9g; Sodium: 291mg

BAKED BUTTER BEANS

GLUTEN-FREE, NUT-FREE, SOY-FREE

Serves 4 / Prep time: 5 minutes / Cook time: 40 minutes

When I was growing up, baked beans were a side dish, not an entrée, and they usually contained bacon. As I morphed from vegetarian to vegan and discovered that beans are the real deal for any meal, I immediately started playing with baked bean recipes. This version of a baked bean is a nod to the gigante beans popular in Greek restaurants. Those special beans are hard to find, so I use butter beans (or other white beans) and use oregano, parsley, and black pepper to preserve the Mediterranean flavor profile.

2 (15-ounce) cans butter beans, rinsed and drained

1 small onion, cut into half-moon slices (see page 6)

1 teaspoon minced garlic (1 clove)

1 (8-ounce) can tomato sauce

2 teaspoons olive oil

1 teaspoon dried oregano

1 teaspoon dried parsley

1 teaspoon salt

½ teaspoon black pepper

1. Preheat the oven to 350°F.

2. Place the beans in a 1½- or 2-quart casserole dish. Add the onion, garlic, tomato sauce, olive oil, oregano, parsley, salt, and pepper. Combine well.

3. Bake until bubbling around the edges, about 40 minutes.

Substitution Tip: Great northern and cannellini beans stand in well for butter beans.

Per serving: Calories: 255; Total fat: 3g; Total carbs: 44g; Fiber: 14g; Sugar: 8g; Protein: 15g; Sodium: 595mg

TOFU SCALLOPED POTATOES

GLUTEN-FREE, NUT-FREE

Serves 4 / Prep time: 15 minutes / Cook time: About 1 hour

Scalloped potatoes were always served as a side dish for our big Sunday dinner, but I made a balanced meal out of them in this recipe. Think of it as a casserole Buddha bowl: we've got our legumes (tofu), starch (potatoes), and greens (spinach). Super-easy, this is one of the longer-cooking recipes in the book, so use that baking time to slice, dice, and prep for other recipes for the week.

Nonstick vegetable oil spray

¼ cup vegan butter

¼ cup chopped yellow or sweet onion

1 pound russet potatoes, unpeeled, sliced about ⅛ inch thick

1 cup shredded vegan cheddar cheese

8 ounces (3 cups tightly packed) spinach

1 cup chopped mushrooms (shiitake or baby bella)

1 cup silken extra-firm tofu (about 6 ounces)

½ cup vegan sour cream (or Simple Vegan Sour Cream, page 124)

¼ cup water

½ teaspoon salt

1 teaspoon paprika

½ teaspoon black pepper

1. Preheat the oven to 350°F. Spray a 9-by-13-inch baking dish with nonstick vegetable oil spray.

2. In a small saucepan over medium-high heat, melt the vegan butter. Add the onion and sauté until it softens, about 3 minutes. Remove the pan from the heat.

3. Layer the sliced potatoes in the prepared baking dish. Spread the vegan cheese evenly over the potatoes. Arrange the spinach over the cheese. Pour the melted butter and onion over the spinach.

4. In a blender or food processor, process the mushrooms, tofu, vegan sour cream, water, and salt together until the mixture is creamy and pourable, 20 to 30 seconds. Pour over the potatoes and spinach. Sprinkle the paprika and pepper evenly over the casserole.

5. Bake until golden brown, about 1 hour. Serve immediately.

Make It Ahead: This can be assembled up to 3 days in advance; cover and refrigerate until ready to bake.

Per serving: Calories: 570; Total fat: 48g; Total carbs: 33g; Fiber: 2g; Sugar: 3g; Protein: 6g; Sodium: 1256mg

SPANISH QUINOA CASSEROLE

GLUTEN-FREE OPTION, NUT-FREE, OIL-FREE OPTION, SOY-FREE

Serves 4 / Prep time: 10 minutes / Cook time: 35 minutes

Here's a protein-rich version of Spanish rice. Baking gives it a really lovely, creamy texture, and the quinoa makes it a healthy meal. Enjoy it as is, with a side of steamed vegetables, or use it as a filling for tacos.

Nonstick vegetable oil spray

1 teaspoon olive oil

½ cup finely chopped onion (yellow, white, or sweet)

2 teaspoons minced garlic (2 cloves)

1 tablespoon chopped jalapeño pepper (fresh or jarred)

1 cup quinoa

2¼ cups hot water

2 teaspoons tomato paste

1 cup chopped tomato

½ teaspoon ground cumin

½ teaspoon paprika (any kind)

½ teaspoon chili powder

¼ teaspoon salt

1. Preheat the oven to 375°F. Spray a 9-by-13-inch baking dish with nonstick vegetable oil spray.

2. In a large skillet over medium-high heat, heat the oil. Sauté the onion, garlic, and jalapeño. Cook until the vegetables begin to soften, about 3 minutes. Transfer to the casserole dish. Add the quinoa, hot water, tomato paste, chopped tomato, cumin, paprika, chili powder, and salt. Stir to combine well.

3. Cover the dish with aluminum foil and bake until bubbling around the edges, about 30 minutes.

4. Remove from the oven and let rest for 5 minutes before fluffing with a fork.

Gluten-free option: Use gluten-free nonstick spray.

Oil-free option: Use a nonstick pan instead of nonstick vegetable oil spray and use 2 teaspoons water or vegetable broth instead of the oil to sauté.

Per serving: Calories: 188; Total fat: 4g; Total carbs: 32g; Fiber: 4g; Sugar: 2g; Protein: 7g; Sodium: 157mg

COLLARD GREEN BEAN BAKE

GLUTEN-FREE, NUT-FREE, SOY-FREE

Serves 4 / Prep time: 10 minutes / Cook time: 20 minutes

If you're like me, once you started eating vegetarian and vegan, you branched out on food choices. Collard greens are common in Southern cooking, often with meat, but they never made it to our dinner table in rural Illinois. I learned about them one New Year's Eve (see Lucky Beans and Greens, page 117) and they quickly became a leafy-green staple. Since we are making beans without meat, the balsamic vinegar brings in the savory, umami flavor.

2 (15-ounce) cans cannellini beans, drained and rinsed

4 cups tightly packed stemmed and shredded collard greens

1 large red bell pepper, seeded and diced

1 large yellow bell pepper, seeded and diced

¼ cup balsamic vinegar

1 teaspoon olive oil

1 teaspoon dried thyme

1 teaspoon dried rosemary

½ teaspoon salt

½ teaspoon black pepper

1. Preheat the oven to 425°F. Line a large baking sheet with parchment paper.

2. In a large bowl, combine the beans, collard greens, bell peppers, vinegar, oil, thyme, rosemary, salt, and black pepper. Transfer to the baking sheet and arrange in an even layer.

3. Bake until the peppers are tender and the collard greens are browned and crisped, about 20 minutes, using tongs at 10 minutes to shake and move everything around for even cooking.

Ingredient Tip: Low in calories and high in calcium, B vitamins, and fiber, collard greens are my obsession. I often buy them bagged and pre-shredded; however, they are very simple to prepare: Lay the collard leaves flat and stacked. Roll them and then cut crosswise into thin shreds. I add shredded collards to soups, salads, savory oats, and more.

Per serving: Calories: 287; Total fat: 3g; Total carbs: 51g; Fiber: 17g; Sugar: 2g; Protein: 18g; Sodium: 312mg

ROASTED KABOCHA SQUASH WITH CHICKPEAS

GLUTEN-FREE, NUT-FREE, OIL-FREE OPTION, SOY-FREE

Serves 4 / Prep time: 10 minutes / Cook time: 35 to 40 minutes

I love winter squash—acorn, butternut, and pumpkin—and I really love kabocha squash. It's a squat little Japanese pumpkin that cooks up quicker than some other squashes, and the skin is edible. Serve the roasted squash wedges and chickpeas over a bed of greens for a salad, or roll up in a tortilla for a super-healthy wrap.

2 (15-ounce) cans chickpeas

1 kabocha squash (2 to 3 pounds)

2 tablespoons olive oil or 2 tablespoons aquafaba (the liquid in a chickpea can), divided

½ teaspoon salt

¼ teaspoon black pepper

2 teaspoons smoked paprika

2 teaspoons garlic powder

1. Preheat the oven to 400°F. Line a medium baking sheet with parchment paper.

2. Open both cans of chickpeas and drain (if making this recipe oil-free, reserve the liquid, called aquafaba, in a small bowl). Transfer the chickpeas to a medium bowl.

3. Wash the squash very well. Cut the squash in half. Remove the seeds with a spoon and discard. Remove the stem and then slice each half lengthwise to create 1-inch-thick wedges. Place the wedges on the baking sheet. Drizzle 1 tablespoon of the olive oil over the squash (or 1 tablespoon aquafaba). Toss with tongs to coat all sides. Sprinkle with salt and pepper. Bake for 20 minutes.

4. While the squash bakes, add the remaining 1 tablespoon olive oil (or aquafaba), paprika, and garlic powder to the bowl with the chickpeas. Toss gently, coating well.

5. Remove the sheet pan from the oven. Flip the squash over and pour the chickpeas onto the sheet pan, spreading them into a single layer around the squash. Bake until chickpeas are just beginning to brown and the squash is tender, 15 to 20 minutes more.

Substitution Tip: Play with flavor profiles. Use a total of 4 teaspoons of ground spices; consider using a Japanese 7-spice blend with ground ginger and shichimi togarashi or an Indian-inspired version with curry powder, turmeric, and garam masala.

Oil-free option: Use aquafaba instead of the oil as indicated in the recipe.

Per serving: Calories: 417; Total fat: 11g; Total carbs: 65g; Fiber: 16g; Sugar: 16g; Protein: 18g; Sodium: 303mg

ROASTED JAPANESE YAMS AND TEMPEH

GLUTEN-FREE OPTION, NUT-FREE, OIL-FREE OPTION

Serves 4 / Prep time: 10 minutes / Cook time: 25 minutes

One of the great things about exploring vegan cooking is that we can add variety to many of the ingredients we use. We're all pretty familiar with russet, red, and sweet potatoes. But how about trying Japanese yams? While they may sound exotic, they are actually available at most neighborhood grocery stores and box stores like Walmart. And since we're trying an Asian sweet potato, let's use an Asian flavor profile. In the future, you can follow this process and swap out the sweet potato and play around with spices to create other flavor profiles, such as Spanish, Indian, or Mediterranean.

2 (8-ounce) packages tempeh, cut into a total of 16 cubes

¼ cup soy sauce or tamari

2 tablespoons unseasoned rice vinegar

2 teaspoons sesame oil

2 teaspoons ground ginger

2 large Japanese yams (about 2 pounds), unpeeled, cut into 1½-inch cubes

1 teaspoon white or black pepper

1 tablespoon sesame seeds

1. Preheat the oven to 425°F. Line a large baking sheet with parchment paper.

2. Place the tempeh in a shallow dish.

3. In a small bowl whisk together the soy sauce, vinegar, sesame oil, and ginger. Pour over the tempeh.

4. Put the sweet potato cubes on the prepared sheet pan. Sprinkle with the pepper. Pour the tempeh and marinade over the yams and toss to combine and coat with the mixture. Spread into a single layer.

5. Bake for 12 minutes. Remove the pan from the oven and, with a spatula or tongs, rotate and flip the tempeh and potato pieces. Bake until the potatoes are tender, about another 12 minutes.

6. Transfer the yams and tempeh to a large serving bowl, sprinkle with the sesame seeds, and serve.

Ingredient Tip: If you prefer, you can also use a regular sweet potato, which will be sweeter and softer than the Japanese yam.

Make It Ahead: The longer tempeh marinates, the more tender it is. Prepare the marinade, pour it in a plastic bag or shallow container, and add the cubed tempeh. Store in the refrigerator for up to 3 days before roasting.

Gluten-free option: Use gluten-free tamari instead of soy sauce.

Oil-free option: Substitute vegetable broth for the sesame oil in the marinade.

Per serving: Calories: 532; Total fat: 16g; Total carbs: 77g; Fiber: 10g; Sugar: 1g; Protein: 26g; Sodium: 803mg

SHEET PAN POTA-CHOS

GLUTEN-FREE OPTION, NUT-FREE, SOY-FREE OPTION

Serves 4 / Prep time: 10 minutes / Cook time: 50 minutes

My husband and I have yet to meet a potato we didn't love. We pressure cook them; we air fry them; we roast them. Potatoes are life. So, it should be no surprise that one night when we were tossing around the idea of having nachos for dinner, we thought potatoes *as nachos* sounded even better. We were right. This recipe is definitely easy, just a bit longer due to the roasting, but it's worth the wait!

1½ pounds russet potatoes, unpeeled, cut into ½-inch dice

Nonstick vegetable oil spray

1 teaspoon chili powder

½ teaspoon cayenne pepper

½ teaspoon salt

1 (15-ounce) can pinto beans, drained and rinsed

1 large red bell pepper, seeded and diced

1 large yellow bell pepper, seeded and diced

1 cup shredded vegan pepper jack cheese (optional)

2 cups shredded lettuce

1 cup cherry tomatoes, halved

½ cup chopped scallions

¼ cup chopped fresh cilantro

Vegan sour cream (or Simple Vegan Sour Cream, page 124) (optional)

Salsa (optional)

1. Preheat the oven to 425°F. Line a large baking sheet with parchment paper.

2. Put the potatoes in a large bowl and spritz once or twice with the nonstick vegetable oil spray. Sprinkle with the chili powder, cayenne, and salt and mix until the potatoes are evenly coated with the seasonings. Arrange in a single layer on the prepared baking sheet. Bake until the potatoes are nearly tender, about 40 minutes, stirring after 20 minutes.

3. Remove from the oven and pull the parchment paper out from under the potatoes. Layer the beans over the potatoes, then the bell peppers, then the shredded cheese (if using). Return to the oven and bake until the potatoes are tender and, if using cheese, the cheese is soft (possibly "melted," in that vegan cheese way) and browning, another 7 to 10 minutes.

4. Cover the pota-chos with the lettuce, tomatoes, scallions, and cilantro. Add a few dollops of vegan sour cream and salsa (if using) and dive in.

Substitution Tip: Want your nachos the way you know and love them? Skip the potatoes. Simply cover an unlined sheet pan with corn tortilla chips. Add the beans, peppers, and cheese and bake at 425°F for 10 to 12 minutes. Then add all the toppings!

Gluten-free option: Use gluten-free cooking spray.

Soy-free option: Omit the vegan sour cream.

Per serving: Calories: 287; Total fat: 2g; Total carbs: 58g; Fiber: 14g; Sugar: 6g; Protein: 12g; Sodium: 316mg

MUSHROOM STROGANOFF BAKE

GLUTEN-FREE OPTION, NUT-FREE, SOY-FREE OPTION

Serves 4 / Prep time: 15 minutes / Cook time: 48 minutes

In my pre-vegan days, beef stroganoff at my house was egg noodles, beef, and cream of mushroom soup (instead of sour cream or heavy cream). This version is healthier, using meaty mushrooms and almond milk. The prep is fast and simple because the pasta cooks with the sauce. Use the bake time to pour a glass of wine, cuddle with your kids or cats, and kick up your feet while you wait for a satisfying dinner that hits all the right notes.

2 large portobello caps

1 tablespoon vegan butter

1 small yellow or sweet onion, diced

1 tablespoon minced garlic (3 cloves)

½ teaspoon salt

¼ teaspoon black pepper

8 ounces fusilli pasta

1 cup beef-style vegan broth or vegetable broth

1 cup almond milk

1. Preheat the oven to 400°F.

2. Destem the portobello mushrooms, if necessary, and slice lengthwise. Then chop each slice into ½-inch pieces.

3. In a Dutch oven over medium-high heat, melt the vegan butter, then add the onion and garlic and sauté until the onion softens, about 3 minutes. Add the mushrooms and sauté until tender, another 3 minutes. Add the salt, pepper, fusilli, broth, and milk. Stir well.

4. Cover and transfer the Dutch oven to the oven. Bake until the pasta is tender, about 40 minutes.

Substitution Tip: This is a soy-free recipe if you opt for non-soy butter. But if you're cool with soy, consider using soy milk instead of almond milk and add a teaspoon of soy sauce instead of salt. Why? One word: umami!

Soy-free option: Use soy-free vegan butter.

Gluten-free option: Use gluten-free fusilli.

Per serving: Calories: 277; Total fat: 4g; Total carbs: 48g; Fiber: 4g; Sugar: 3g; Protein: 11g; Sodium: 415mg

SHEET PAN LASAGNA

More Sauce + Add veggies!

GLUTEN-FREE OPTION, NUT-FREE

Serves 8 / Prep time: 10 minutes / Cook time: 30 minutes

If you're not eschewing carbs, this pasta noodle version is for you. This is the recipe I make when my non-vegan friends and family are visiting. You can make it super-speedy with jarred sauce, prepared vegan ricotta, and canned or jarred mushrooms. You can slow it down and go a bit more wholesome by taking the time to make the Marinara Sauce on page 129 and the Ch-ofu Ricotta on page 125. Cook's choice!

1 (24-ounce) jar marinara sauce (or 3 cups Marinara Sauce, page 129), divided

1 (8-ounce) box oven-ready (no-boil) vegan lasagna noodles

4 cups sliced mushrooms

2 cups vegan ricotta (or Ch-ofu Ricotta, page 125)

¼ cup water

1 cup shredded vegan mozzarella cheese

Add vegs

1. Preheat the oven to 375°F.

2. Onto a medium baking sheet, pour 1½ cups of the marinara sauce and spread evenly with a spatula or spoon. Place 6 lasagna noodles over the sauce, covering the pan. Distribute the sliced mushrooms over the noodles and then dollop on the vegan ricotta. Use a spatula to spread the ricotta to cover everything. Layer over another 6 sheets of pasta. Spread the remaining 1½ cups tomato sauce over the noodles. Pour the water over everything. Sprinkle the shredded vegan mozzarella over the top.

3. Bake until the sauce is bubbling and the noodles are tender, about 30 minutes.

Ingredient Tip: My two go-to vegan ricotta brands at the local grocery stores are Tofutti Better Than Ricotta and Kite Hill Ricotta.
Gluten-free option: Use gluten-free oven-ready lasagna noodles.

Per serving: Calories: 302; Total fat: 7g; Total carbs: 47g; Fiber: 18g; Sugar: 8g; Protein: 18g; Sodium: 291mg

Edamame Sushi Rice, page 115

7

No-Pressure Pressure Cooking

This chapter is for you pressure cooker, multicooker, and Instant Pot® fans! In this chapter you're going to make great food fast and under pressure. Please do remember, though, that in addition to the pressure-cooking time noted in the recipe, the pot must first come up to pressure and then come down. I'm managing expectations because the cooking time is slightly deceptive. But here's what isn't deceptive: If you're using an electric device, you get to "set it and forget it" for these one-pot recipes!

PRESSURE-COOKING POINTERS

A call for quick release means *you* move the lever on your multicooker from sealing to vent (or, if using a stovetop pressure cooker, set the pot under running cold water in the sink) until all the pressure releases and the pin drops, allowing you to unlock the lid.

Natural release means you don't do anything. Take the pot off the heat if it's a stovetop unit, or turn the pot off if it's electric, and leave it until the pin drops on its own and you can unlock the lid. The only exception is if a recipe calls for natural release for a specified number of minutes. If the pin hasn't dropped by then, quick release the remaining pressure as outlined above.

If you don't have a pressure cooker, here's a general way to adapt these recipes:

- Follow the recipe until it's time to set up for pressure cooking. Here you'll bring the food up to a boil, cover, reduce the heat to simmer, and cook until done (usually three times longer than the pressure-cooking time, but you'll want to test to ensure it is fully cooked).
- You may need more liquid than is called for in the recipe, so keep an eye on that.

SAVORY OATS

GLUTEN-FREE OPTION, NUT-FREE, OIL-FREE OPTION, SOY-FREE

Serves 4 / Prep time: 5 minutes / Cook time: 3 minutes to sauté, 5 minutes at high pressure, natural release

Here's a great way to use some of your prepped mirepoix ingredients. I almost always use a simple sauté when pressure cooking because it gets the pot hot, which means it will come to pressure quicker. This recipe is great on its own. And it's also a great foundation for building flavor. You can add Italian, Indian, Southwestern, Japanese, or Mediterranean spices for a bit more complexity.

1 teaspoon vegan butter

½ cup diced sweet or yellow onion

¼ cup diced carrot

¼ cup diced celery

¾ cup rolled oats

2 cups vegetable broth

½ cup water

½ teaspoon salt

¼ cup nutritional yeast

¼ teaspoon black pepper

2 to 4 cups baby spinach, arugula, or other quick-cooking leafy green (optional)

1. In a pressure cooker, combine the vegan butter, onion, carrot, and celery. Select Sauté for an electric pot, or sauté over medium-high heat until the onion softens, about 3 minutes. Add water or vegetable broth if it begins to stick. Stir in the rolled oats, broth, water, and salt.

2. Lock the lid. Select high pressure and set for 5 minutes if using an electric pressure cooker. If using a stovetop pressure cooker, increase the heat to bring to high pressure, then maintain high pressure for 5 minutes. Use a natural release.

3. Stir in the nutritional yeast, pepper, and greens (if using) and serve.

Substitution Tip: If you want an even creamier bowl of savory oats, use ½ cup plant-based milk instead of water.

Gluten-free option: Use certified gluten-free oats.

Oil-free option: Use 2 teaspoons water or vegetable broth instead of the vegan butter to sauté.

Per serving: Calories: 156; Total fat: 4g; Total carbs: 20g; Fiber: 6g; Sugar: 2g; Protein: 13g; Sodium: 500mg

FAST AND EASY FRUIT "COMPOTE"

GLUTEN-FREE, NUT-FREE, OIL-FREE, SOY-FREE

Serves 4 / Prep time: 10 minutes / Cook time: 3 minutes at high pressure, quick release

Culinary cheating has been the name of my game since going vegan. This recipe is a perfect example. It's not quite compote and it's definitely not jam (because I'm avoiding thickeners). It *is* a great way to use fruit that you didn't quite get to in time and don't want to throw out. It's fantastic stirred into oatmeal or spooned over vegan ice cream. And, what's better than something that can be served for both breakfast and dessert? Nothing.

2 cups diced unpeeled apples

2 cups diced unpeeled pears

½ cup blueberries

1 teaspoon ground cinnamon

1 teaspoon ground ginger

½ cup water

2 tablespoons lemon juice (1 medium lemon)

2 tablespoons agave syrup or ¼ cup sugar (optional)

1. In a pressure cooker, stir together the apples, pears, blueberries, cinnamon, ginger, and water. Lock the lid. Select high pressure and set for 3 minutes if using an electric pressure cooker. If using a stovetop pressure cooker, increase the heat to bring to high pressure, then maintain high pressure for 3 minutes. Use a quick release.

2. Mash the fruit with a potato masher while adding the lemon juice, leaving it a bit chunky. Taste before determining if you want to add agave or sugar. Enjoy warm or cold.

Ingredient Tip: Use any type of apple or pear that you enjoy. I'm partial to Granny Smith apples with Bosc pears, but it's cook's choice!

Make It Slower: To make this in a pot on your stove, follow step 1 and bring to a boil, cover, reduce the heat to low, and simmer until the apple and pear are tender, 15 to 20 minutes. Resume at step 2.

Make It Ahead: This can be prepared up to 5 days in advance; refrigerate in an airtight container.

Per serving: Calories: 115; Total fat: 0g; Total carbs: 30g; Fiber: 7g; Sugar: 20g; Protein: 1g; Sodium: 4mg

WARM CABBAGE SALAD

GLUTEN-FREE, NUT-FREE, OIL-FREE, SOY-FREE

Serves 4 / Prep time: 10 minutes / Cook time: 3 minutes at low pressure, quick release

My grandfather used to make delicious German potato salad and a variety of cabbage slaw dishes. (Hey, maybe that's how I grew to love umami?) I find a warm cabbage dish delights my palate while nourishing my body. Lovely as a side, you can even use this salad as the "green" in a beans, greens, and grains hippie bowl. Bonus: The leftovers are delicious cold.

¼ cup water

¼ cup apple cider vinegar

½ teaspoon dried dill

½ teaspoon dry mustard

½ teaspoon sea salt

¼ teaspoon black pepper

1 large pear, cored and cut into matchsticks

1 large red apple, cored and cut into matchsticks

1 large carrot, cut into matchsticks

4 scallions (white and green parts), chopped

1 small head green or red cabbage, cored and shredded

1. In a pressure cooker, stir together the water, vinegar, dill, mustard, salt, and pepper. Add the pear, apple, carrot, and scallions and stir. Place the cabbage on top. Do not stir.

2. Lock the lid. Select low pressure and set for 3 minutes if using an electric pressure cooker. If using a stovetop pressure cooker, increase the heat to bring to low pressure, then maintain low pressure for 3 minutes. Use a quick release.

3. Stir everything together and serve.

Ingredient Tip: I often double this recipe for potlucks and I'll use both a green and a red head of cabbage to make a vibrantly colorful dish.

Per serving: Calories: 124; Total fat: 1g; Total carbs: 30g; Fiber: 9g; Sugar: 18g; Protein: 4g; Sodium: 292mg

PAPRIKA POTATO SOUP

GLUTEN-FREE, NUT-FREE, OIL-FREE OPTION

Serves 4 / Prep time: 5 minutes / Cook time: 6 minutes at low pressure, quick release

In every cookbook I've written, I include a recipe with a Hungarian twist in honor of my husband and my mother-in-law. There's so much umami going on—from the spices to the sauerkraut—and it cooks up even faster because we're using canned beans.

2 large russet potatoes (about 20 ounces total), unpeeled and diced

1 (15-ounce) can chickpeas, drained but not rinsed

1 (14-ounce) can sauerkraut, drained

1 cup diced tomato (about 1 medium tomato)

1 tablespoon minced garlic (3 cloves)

1 tablespoon sweet Hungarian paprika

1 teaspoon smoked paprika

4 cups beef-style vegan broth or vegetable broth

½ cup vegan sour cream (or Simple Vegan Sour Cream, page 124)

½ teaspoon black pepper

1. In a pressure cooker, stir together the potatoes, chickpeas, sauerkraut, tomato, garlic, sweet and smoked paprikas, and broth.

2. Lock the lid. Select low pressure and set for 6 minutes if using an electric pressure cooker. If using a stovetop pressure cooker, increase the heat to bring to low pressure, then maintain low pressure for 6 minutes. Use a quick release.

3. Stir in the vegan sour cream and pepper and serve.

Substitution Tip: I love chickpeas in this soup, but I have made it with pinto, cannellini, and cranberry beans. All good!

Oil-free option: Use Simple Vegan Sour Cream.

Per serving: Calories: 357; Total fat: 8g; Total carbs: 61g; Fiber: 15g; Sugar: 11g; Protein: 13g; Sodium: 705mg

PERFECT PASTA UNDER PRESSURE

GLUTEN-FREE OPTION, NUT-FREE, OIL-FREE OPTION, SOY-FREE

Serves 4 / Prep time: 5 minutes / Cook time: 6 minutes to sauté, 3 to 5 minutes at low pressure, quick release

I've been amazed by the number of people ready to return their multicooker because all they wanted was one-pot pasta and it never worked. The number one culprit? Scorching. Tomatoes are thick and sugary and they can burn or scorch under pressure. But never fear, there's a recipe for success—just follow my 1:1:1 formula—one part pasta, one part water, one part pasta sauce—and *do not stir* the sauce in before locking the lid!

2 teaspoons olive oil

1 small yellow or sweet onion, diced

½ cup diced carrot

½ cup diced celery

4 teaspoons minced garlic

1 teaspoon dried basil

1 teaspoon dried oregano

1 teaspoon red pepper flakes

8 ounces spelt pasta or gluten-free pasta

1 cup (8 ounces) water

1 cup (8 ounces) marinara sauce (jarred, canned, or Marinara Sauce, page 129)

1. In a pressure cooker, combine the olive oil, onion, carrot, celery, and garlic. Select Sauté for an electric pot or sauté over medium-high heat until the onion softens, about 3 minutes. Add the basil, oregano, and red pepper flakes and sauté 3 minutes longer. Add the pasta and water and stir well. Pour the marinara sauce over the top; *do not stir*.

2. Lock the lid. Select low pressure and set for 3 to 5 minutes (see Pick the Right Pasta, below) if using an electric cooker. If using a stovetop cooker, increase the heat to bring to high pressure, then maintain high pressure for 3 to 5 minutes. Use a quick release. Stir well and serve.

Gluten-free option: Use gluten-free pasta.
Oil-free option: Use 1 tablespoon water or vegetable broth instead of the oil to sauté.

Per serving: Calories: 267; Total fat: 4g; Total carbs: 49g; Fiber: 7g; Sugar: 4g; Protein: 9g; Sodium: 139mg

PICK THE RIGHT PASTA

Pasta often does not perform well under pressure, but a whole-grain one—such as one made from spelt—or a gluten-free pasta made from corn or quinoa will. The pressure-cooking time will vary with the pasta you choose. My general rule is to cut the cook time suggested on the package in half. For instance, if the package states 6 to 8 minutes cooking time, opt for 3 minutes (half of the lowest suggested time)—it's better to undercook the pasta than overcook it; you can always sauté the pasta uncovered in the pressure cooker after releasing pressure if it's a little underdone. And remember: always use low pressure and a quick release.

SPICY QUINOA PILAF

GLUTEN-FREE, NUT-FREE, OIL-FREE OPTION, SOY-FREE

Serves 4 / Prep time: 5 minutes / Cook time: 3 minutes to sauté, plus 1 minute at high pressure, natural release

One-minute quinoa, y'all! Okay, not really because obviously it has to come to pressure first, but, yes, it only cooks for 1 minute. Protein-rich quinoa makes this dish a meal in its own right (just serve it up hot or cold over steamed or raw veggies), but served up spicy, this is also a terrific taco filling or topping for tostadas.

1 teaspoon olive oil

½ cup chopped red onion

½ cup chopped red bell pepper

½ cup chopped green bell pepper

1 tablespoon chopped jalapeño (or serrano) pepper

1 cup quinoa

1½ cups vegetable broth

½ teaspoon chili powder or chipotle powder

½ teaspoon ground cumin

½ teaspoon sea salt

¼ teaspoon black pepper

1 small tomato, chopped

1. In a pressure cooker, combine the olive oil, onion, and peppers. Select Sauté for an electric pot or sauté over medium-high heat until the onion begins to soften, about 3 minutes. Add water or vegetable broth if it begins to stick. Stir in the quinoa, broth, chili powder, cumin, salt, and pepper. Drop the chopped tomato on top, and *do not stir*.

2. Lock the lid. Select high pressure and set for 1 minute if using an electric pressure cooker. If using a stovetop pressure cooker, increase the heat to bring to high pressure, then maintain high pressure for 1 minute. Use a natural release.

3. Fluff the quinoa with a fork before serving.

Ingredient Tip: Jarred jalapeños are a fine substitute for the fresh pepper.

Oil-free option: Use 2 teaspoons water instead of the oil to sauté.

Per serving: Calories: 188; Total fat: 2g; Total carbs: 32g; Fiber: 4g; Sugar: 3g; Protein: 7g; Sodium: 243mg

EDAMAME SUSHI RICE

GLUTEN-FREE, OIL-FREE

Serves 4 / Prep time: 5 minutes / Cook time: 6 minutes at high pressure, quick release

Combining beans and grains into one pot under pressure is a dream come true: two powerful plant-based foods serving up protein, fiber, and nutrients and forming the tasty base of a full and balanced meal. The trick is getting the cooking times just right—you need a grain and bean that cook at the same pressure and have relatively close cooking times. That's why this sushi rice and frozen edamame combo works so well.

2½ cups water

1½ cups sushi rice (short-grain Japanese rice)

1 cup frozen shelled edamame (don't defrost)

1 teaspoon mirin or white wine

1 teaspoon unseasoned rice vinegar

½ teaspoon dulse flakes (optional)

1. In a pressure cooker, combine the water, rice, and edamame. Lock the lid. Select high pressure and set for 6 minutes if using an electric pressure cooker. If using a stovetop pressure cooker, increase the heat to bring to high pressure, then maintain high pressure for 6 minutes.

2. Use a quick release but *do not uncover*. Keep the lid locked in place for 5 minutes.

3. Remove the lid, sprinkle the rice with the mirin, vinegar, and dulse flakes (if using) while fluffing the rice with a fork, and serve.

Per serving: Calories: 289; Total fat: 2g; Total carbs: 60g; Fiber: 3g; Sugar: 1g; Protein: 7g; Sodium: 18mg

MAKE SUSHI ROLLS FOR LUNCH OR A BOWL FOR DINNER

This simple, protein-packed sticky rice is incredibly versatile!

- Slice carrots, scallions, and bell peppers into sticks and line them up with about ¼ cup Edamame Sushi Rice on a nori sheet. Add a slice of avocado. Repeat to make one more roll. Roll them up, slice them, and you've got vegan sushi! (It is excellent with Macro Miso Soup, page 42.)
- Make a deconstructed Buddha Bowl. Chop all the veggies mentioned above and cube the avocado. Serve over 1 cup of the Edamame Sushi Rice, then crumble a nori sheet over the top. Drizzle with a little soy or peanut sauce and serve.

CHIPOTLE LENTILS

GLUTEN-FREE, NUT-FREE, OIL-FREE, SOY-FREE

Serves 4 / Prep time: 10 minutes / Cook time: 5 minutes to simmer, 10 minutes at high pressure, natural release

I love to have a heavily spiced bean at the ready for anything. These flavorful lentils can be served in toasted pita bread, over baked or mashed potatoes, as taco filling, or even as a substitute for cheese and tomato sauce on pizza. To save you a little money, it uses spices that give you the flavor of adobo sauce without having to buy it.

2 cups water

1 tablespoon tomato paste

1 tablespoon cider vinegar

1 teaspoon chipotle powder (or smoked paprika)

1 teaspoon ground cumin

½ teaspoon garlic powder

½ teaspoon dried basil or oregano

1 cup dried brown lentils

¼ teaspoon salt

1. In a pressure cooker, combine the water, tomato paste, vinegar, chipotle powder, cumin, garlic powder, and dried basil. Select Sauté for an electric pot or set a stovetop pressure cooker over medium-high heat and bring to a simmer, about 5 minutes. Add the lentils and stir well.

2. Lock the lid. Select high pressure and set for 10 minutes if using an electric pressure cooker. If using a stovetop pressure cooker, increase the heat to bring to high pressure, then maintain high pressure for 10 minutes. Use a natural release.

3. Stir in the salt and serve.

Add Even More Protein: Turn these Chipotle Lentils into a dish similar to what you can find at the Chipotle chain restaurants: Take half a batch of the Barbecue Tofu (page 50) and crumble it. Add it to the lentils when stirring in the salt. So good!

Per serving: Calories: 178; Total fat: 1g; Total carbs: 30g; Fiber: 15g; Sugar: 2g; Protein: 13g; Sodium: 155mg

LUCKY BEANS AND GREENS

GLUTEN-FREE, NUT-FREE, SOY-FREE, OIL-FREE OPTION

Serves 6 / Prep time: 10 minutes / Cook time: 3 minutes to sauté, 10 minutes at high pressure, natural release

Black-eyed peas and collard greens are a New Year's Day tradition on many Southern tables. Known as Hoppin' John, the lore is that black-eyed peas bring good luck and collard greens, the color of money, bring prosperity. This vegan version skips ham and pork and goes right to plant-based meatiness (umami) with mushrooms and liquid smoke.

1 teaspoon olive oil

1 tablespoon minced garlic (3 cloves)

1 cup diced yellow or sweet onion

1 cup coarsely chopped mushrooms (shiitake, cremini, oyster, or baby bella)

1 tablespoon smoked paprika

1 teaspoon ground cinnamon

1 teaspoon ground cumin

½ teaspoon ground coriander

¼ teaspoon liquid smoke

2 cups dried black-eyed peas, rinsed and drained

2 cups water

4 large collard green leaves, destemmed and cut into strips (see Ingredient Tip)

1 (8-ounce) can tomato sauce

½ teaspoon sea salt

¼ teaspoon black pepper

1. In a pressure cooker, combine the olive oil, garlic, onion, and mushrooms. Select Sauté for an electric pot or sauté over medium-high heat until the onion softens, about 3 minutes. Stir in the paprika, cinnamon, cumin, coriander, and liquid smoke until well combined. Add the black-eyed peas and water and stir. Place the collard green strips on top and pour the tomato sauce over everything. *Do not stir.*

2. Lock the lid. Select high pressure and set for 10 minutes if using an electric pressure cooker. If using a stovetop pressure cooker, increase the heat to bring to high pressure, then maintain high pressure for 10 minutes. Use a natural release.

3. Stir in the salt and pepper (add more to taste if you like) and serve.

Ingredient Tip: Lay the collard leaves flat and stacked. Roll them and then cut crosswise into thin strips.

Oil-free option: Use 2 teaspoons water instead of the oil to sauté.

Per serving: Calories: 197; Total fat: 1g; Total carbs: 47g; Fiber: 20g; Sugar: 3g; Protein: 18g; Sodium: 195mg

ONE-POT HIPPIE BOWL

GLUTEN-FREE, NUT-FREE, OIL-FREE OPTION, SOY-FREE

Serves 4 / Prep time: 5 minutes / Cook time: 3 minutes to sauté, 23 minutes at high pressure, natural release

The formula for a solid hippie bowl (also known as a Buddha bowl): beans, greens, and grains. The technique for combining foods in the pressure cooker or multicooker is to use foods that have nearly the same cooking time. Both formula and technique come together beautifully when you build a meal around brown rice and dried beans, because many dried legumes cook up in 22 to 23 minutes, as does the rice. Serve this with the Mmm Mmm Umami Queso (page 126).

1 teaspoon olive oil

1 small sweet onion, cut into half-moon slices (see page 6)

2 carrots, chopped

1 tablespoon minced garlic (3 cloves)

1 teaspoon ground cumin

½ teaspoon dried oregano

1 cup dried cranberry or pinto beans, rinsed and drained

½ cup brown rice

3 cups water

4 cups bite-size pieces kale (just tear with your hands)

½ teaspoon salt

¼ teaspoon black pepper

1. In a pressure cooker, combine the olive oil, onion, carrots, garlic, cumin, and oregano. Select Sauté for an electric pot or sauté over medium-high heat until the onion softens, about 3 minutes. Stir in the beans, rice, and water. Place the kale on top. *Do not stir.*

2. Lock the lid. Select high pressure and set for 23 minutes if using an electric pressure cooker. If using a stovetop pressure cooker, increase the heat to bring to high pressure, then maintain high pressure for 23 minutes. Use a natural release.

3. Stir the kale into the rice and beans. Stir in the salt and pepper and serve.

Ingredient Tip: I have you setting the kale on top of the food to steam. Yes, it will seem a bit overcooked but it works for this dish because we want tender greens.

Oil-free option: Use 2 teaspoons water instead of the oil to sauté.

Per serving: Calories: 322; Total fat: 3g; Total carbs: 61g; Fiber: 11g; Sugar: 3g; Protein: 15g; Sodium: 355mg

Tzatziki (page 128) with vegetable dippers

8

Kitchen Staples

You can buy a vegan version of most of the recipes in this chapter. But I think these have knockout flavors that you'll want to use often. So why not go for homemade and save some dough and have fresh flavor, to boot? You'll notice that I really focus on protein, too, and for good reason. Sometimes a fast and easy vegan dish can simply be a raw salad or a steamed vegetable. Pour a high-protein sauce over it, and you've got yourself a meal.

EVERYDAY VEGETABLE BROTH

GLUTEN-FREE, NUT-FREE, OIL-FREE, SOY-FREE

Makes about 8 cups / Prep time: 5 minutes / Cook time: 45 minutes

You likely have many of these ingredients around most of the time and that means that any day of the week you could easily pull together a simple, flavorful broth. I love to set my jar of broth on the counter in the evening when cooking or reheating food, spooning broth in as needed. And, of course, this is perfect for any recipe in this book calling for vegetable broth.

8 cups water

4 large carrots, coarsely chopped

4 stalks celery, coarsely chopped

1 cup sliced mushrooms

1 apple (any kind), quartered (include the peel and core)

4 to 6 cloves garlic, unpeeled, halved

1 teaspoon black peppercorns

2 sprigs fresh thyme (or 1 teaspoon dried thyme)

2 bay leaves

1. In a large pot, combine the water, carrots, celery, mushrooms, apple, garlic, peppercorns, thyme, and bay leaves. Bring to a low boil over high heat. Once boiling, reduce the heat to low and simmer for 40 minutes.

2. Strain the broth through a fine-mesh strainer or cheesecloth and discard the solids.

Make It Even Faster: Pull out your trusty pressure cooker! Add all the ingredients to a steamer basket and set it in the pot. Lock the lid and cook on high pressure for 15 minutes. Use a natural release. Pull the basket out and you've strained the broth!

Make It Ahead: This can be prepared up to 1 week in advance and refrigerated in an airtight container or frozen in a plastic freezer bag for 3 to 6 months.

Per serving (1 cup): Calories: 40; Total fat: 0g; Total carbs: 8g; Fiber: 2g; Sugar: 4g; Protein: 2g; Sodium: 102mg

OAT MILK

GLUTEN-FREE OPTION, NUT-FREE, OIL-FREE, SOY-FREE

Makes 4 cups / Prep time: 30 to 60 minutes

Plant-based milk is called for frequently in the recipes in this cookbook (and I use it all the time in my vegan cooking at home). You can absolutely buy cold and shelf-stable plant, seed, and nut milks. I certainly do. (I also keep soy milk and coconut milk powders on hand.) But why not quickly whip up fresh oat milk following this simple process?

1 cup rolled oats

4 cups water

1. Into a large bowl, put the oats. Cover with water and soak for 30 to 60 minutes. Rinse and drain the oats and discard the soaking water.

2. In a high-speed blender, combine the soaked oats with the 4 cups fresh cold water. Blend on the highest speed for 1 minute.

3. Pour the milk through a cheesecloth or a nut milk bag into the same bowl used for soaking. Optionally (but highly recommended), do a second strain using a fine strainer from the bowl to a pitcher or container that has an airtight lid.

Ingredient Tip: For sweetened oat milk, add 2 large pitted dates to the blender.

Make It Ahead: This can be prepared up to 5 days in advance; refrigerate in an airtight container.

Gluten-free option: Use certified gluten-free oats.

Per serving (1 cup): Calories: 98; Total fat: 2g; Total carbs: 17g; Fiber: 2g; Sugar: 4g; Protein: 3g; Sodium: 80mg

SIMPLE VEGAN SOUR CREAM

GLUTEN-FREE, NUT-FREE, OIL-FREE

Makes about 2 cups sour cream / Prep time: 5 minutes

Traditional vegan sour cream is soy based and this one is no exception. The creamy blended tofu delivers the texture we love. The simple addition of acidic ingredients—lemon juice and vinegar—provides the tang. Use it as is or customize it to the dish. Making Sheet Pan Pota-chos (page 103)? Add chili powder to taste while blending it. Coconut Curry Soup (page 46)? Add a little turmeric. Have fun with this one!

1 (14-ounce) package firm tofu, drained (not pressed)

¼ cup lemon juice (1 to 2 lemons)

2 tablespoons apple cider vinegar

1 teaspoon minced garlic (1 clove) (optional; see Ingredient Tip)

½ teaspoon salt

In a blender or food processor, place the tofu, lemon juice, vinegar, garlic, and salt and process until creamy.

Ingredient Tip: If making sour cream to use in a variety of dishes, you may want to wait before adding the garlic (if at all), depending upon the recipe you're going to use it with.

Substitution Tip: When preparing this for an Asian-influenced meal such as a dip for the sushi or as a dressing, use 1 teaspoon white or yellow miso instead of the salt.

Make It Ahead: This can be prepared up to 5 days in advance; refrigerate in an airtight container—a glass pint jar is ideal.

Per serving (2 tablespoons): Calories: 20; Total fat: 1g; Total carbs: 1g; Fiber: 0g; Sugar: 0g; Protein: 2g; Sodium: 78mg

CH-OFU RICOTTA

yum!

GLUTEN-FREE, NUT-FREE, OIL-FREE

Makes 2½ cups / Prep time: 5 minutes

This incredibly fast and easy savory vegan ricotta alternative is perfect for both lasagna recipes in this book (pages 71 and 105) and it's also great on toast, pizza, sliced raw vegetables, and crackers. Hey, why not steam spinach and combine it with ricotta for an alt-spinach dip?

1 (12-ounce) package firm tofu, pressed and drained (see page 23)

1 (15-ounce) can chickpeas, drained but not rinsed

½ cup nutritional yeast

2 tablespoons unseasoned rice vinegar

2 teaspoons dried basil

1 teaspoon garlic powder

½ teaspoon salt

In a food processor or blender, combine the tofu, chickpeas, nutritional yeast, vinegar, basil, garlic powder, and salt. Pulse until well mixed, with a creamy, cottage cheese–like consistency.

Make It Ahead: This can be prepared up to 5 days in advance; refrigerate in an airtight container.

Per serving (¼ cup): Calories: 127; Total fat: 3g; Total carbs: 15g; Fiber: 6g; Sugar: 2g; Protein: 12g; Sodium: 127mg

MMM MMM UMAMI QUESO

GLUTEN-FREE OPTION, OIL-FREE OPTION

Makes about 3 cups / Prep time: 5 minutes / Cook time: 10 to 15 minutes

For non-vegans, queso is looked at as a side dish or appetizer. But we plant-inspired folks like a good sauce or dressing on just about anything, so it should be no surprise that I use this version with abandon. I know this one calls for a lot of different spices, but each one brings its own special qualities, resulting in a final flavor you're going to love.

8 ounces sweet potato (about 1 small or one half of a medium sweet potato)

2 cups roasted cashews

¼ cup nutritional yeast

2 teaspoons white or yellow miso

1 teaspoon chipotle powder

1 teaspoon smoked paprika

½ teaspoon turmeric

½ teaspoon garlic powder

½ teaspoon ground cumin

1 cup warm water

1 tablespoon olive oil

1. Leave the skin on the sweet potato and cut into cubes (about 8 pieces). Place in a large pot and add just enough water to cover. Bring to a boil over high heat and let continue to boil until the potato is tender when pierced with a fork, about 15 minutes. Drain the potato, return to the pot, and gently mash with a fork or potato masher (you should have about ½ cup).

2. To a blender or food processor, add the cashews and the mashed potato. Add the nutritional yeast, miso, chipotle powder, paprika, turmeric, garlic powder, cumin, warm water, and oil. Blend to achieve a consistency that is easy to pour but still thick.

Make It Even Faster: Cook the sweet potato in your pressure cooker. Add ½ cup water to the pot and heat while dicing the sweet potato. Add the potato to the pot, lock the lid, and cook on low pressure for 6 minutes. Quick release the steam. Drain the water, mash in the pot, and continue with the directions. Another time-saving tip is to reserve ½ cup mashed sweet potatoes the next time you make them just so you can prepare this.

Make It Ahead: This can be prepared up to 5 days in advance; refrigerate in an airtight container. Reheat gently before serving.

Gluten-free option: Use gluten-free miso.

Oil-free option: Use water instead of the oil for blending.

Per serving (2 tablespoons): Calories: 91; Total fat: 6g; Total carbs: 7g; Fiber: 1g; Sugar: 1g; Protein: 3g; Sodium: 24mg

CASHEW DRESSING

GLUTEN-FREE, OIL-FREE, SOY-FREE

Makes 1 cup / Prep time: 10 minutes

Cashew dressing is great for enhancing a salad, spicing up a steamed vegetable, and adding creaminess to wraps. Though I call for soaking the cashews, it's not necessary when using a high-speed blender like a BlendTec or Vitamix.

½ cup unsalted raw cashews

¼ cup orange juice (or lemon juice)

3 tablespoons sesame seeds

2 teaspoons minced garlic (2 cloves; if using whole, quarter them)

½ teaspoon maple or agave syrup

⅛ to ¼ cup water

A pinch or two salt

1. Cover the cashews with room-temperature water to soak for 20 minutes.

2. Drain the cashews and transfer to a food processor or blender. Add the orange juice, sesame seeds, garlic, and maple syrup. Pulse, adding the water as needed to achieve a creamy salad dressing consistency. Taste before adding salt.

Make It Ahead: This can be prepared up to 5 days in advance; refrigerate in an airtight container.

Per serving (2 tablespoons): Calories: 79; Total fat: 6g; Total carbs: 5g; Fiber: 1g; Sugar: 2g; Protein: 2g; Sodium: 45mg

TZATZIKI

GLUTEN-FREE, NUT-FREE, OIL-FREE

Makes 2 cups / Prep time: 10 minutes

This sauce has Middle Eastern origins. Traditionally made with yogurt, the lemon juice and vinegar provide the tangy flavor we're looking for in combination with the tofu. This is wonderful drizzled over spicy foods (try it on Chana Masala, page 74) but it's great as a snack with raw vegetables or drizzled over a veggie burger or even tacos.

1 small cucumber, unpeeled, cut in half

2 (14-ounce) packages firm tofu, drained

1 large lemon, juiced

2 teaspoons rice vinegar or apple cider vinegar

1 tablespoon water

1 tablespoon chopped fresh dill

¼ teaspoon sea salt

1 small cucumber, unpeeled, cut in half

1. Cut the cucumber in half . Cut one half into a couple of pieces; cut the other half into small dice. Set the dice aside.

2. In a food processor or blender, combine the cucumber pieces, tofu, lemon juice, vinegar, water, dill, and salt. Pulse for about 20 seconds, long enough to blend everything and achieve a thick, yogurtlike consistency. Add more water, if needed. Pour into a large bowl.

3. Add the diced cucumber to the bowl and stir to combine.

4. Pour the tzatziki into an airtight container and refrigerate, ideally one day before using, to let the flavor develop. If you make this on the same day you plan to use it, place it in the freezer 30 minutes before serving.

Make It Ahead: This can be prepared up to 5 days in advance; refrigerate in an airtight container.

Per serving (¼ cup): Calories: 87; Total fat: 4g; Total carbs: 6g; Fiber: 1g; Sugar: 2g; Protein: 9g; Sodium: 74mg

MARINARA SAUCE

GLUTEN-FREE, NUT-FREE, OIL-FREE OPTION, SOY-FREE

Makes 4 cups / Prep time: 5 minutes / Cook time: 35 to 50 minutes

This is a recipe I've used for many years. Using ingredients we almost always have on hand, the flavors are complex but the method is anything but. Marinara sauce isn't just for pasta. It's great over baked potatoes, on crusty bread, and even stirred into a simple soup for a flavor boost.

1 teaspoon olive oil

4 to 6 teaspoons minced garlic (4 to 6 cloves)

1 cup diced yellow or sweet onion

1 teaspoon dried basil

1 teaspoon dried oregano

1 teaspoon dried parsley

1 teaspoon dried thyme

½ teaspoon red pepper flakes

½ teaspoon sugar

½ teaspoon sea salt

¼ teaspoon black pepper

1 (28-ounce) can crushed tomatoes

½ cup vegetable broth

1. In a large saucepan, heat the oil over medium-high heat. Add the garlic and onion and sauté until the onion softens, about 3 minutes. Add the basil, oregano, parsley, thyme, red pepper flakes, sugar, salt, black pepper, tomatoes, and broth. Stir to combine. Bring to a boil.

2. Set the lid askew on top, reduce the heat to low, and simmer for 30 minutes to develop the flavors. It's even better if you can let it simmer for 45 minutes.

Ingredient Tip: For a plant-based version of Bolognese sauce, add 1 (8-ounce) package of tempeh during step 1, crumbling it with a wooden spoon, and double the basil, oregano, parsley, thyme, red pepper flakes, and black pepper.

Make It Ahead: This can be prepared up to 5 days in advance and refrigerated in an airtight container or frozen in a heavy-duty plastic bag for up to 3 months.

Oil-free option: Use 1 tablespoon water instead of the oil to sauté.

Per serving (½ cup): Calories: 57; Total fat: 1g; Total carbs: 10g; Fiber: 4g; Sugar: 6g; Protein: 3g; Sodium: 356mg

PEANUT SAUCE

GLUTEN-FREE OPTION, OIL-FREE

Makes ¾ cup / Prep time: 5 minutes

Peanut sauce is a staple for us. Legume-rich and tasty, it adds protein and flavor to anything, and can be used as a sauce for cooked vegetables, as a condiment for falafel or veggie burgers, and, yes, as a dip for crackers or raw vegetables.

½ cup creamy peanut butter

2 tablespoons
low-sodium tamari

1 tablespoon fresh lime juice

1 (1-inch) piece fresh
ginger, peeled

1 teaspoon minced garlic
(1 clove)

1 teaspoon maple syrup

½ teaspoon chili paste

¼ to ½ cup water

In a food processor or blender, combine the peanut butter, tamari, lime juice, ginger, garlic, maple syrup, and chili paste and blend until smooth. Add water as needed to achieve a thick consistency that is just thin enough to drizzle.

Make It Ahead: This can be prepared up to 5 days in advance; refrigerate in an airtight container.

Gluten-free option: Use a gluten-free tamari.

Per serving (2 tablespoons): Calories: 136; Total fat: 11g; Total carbs: 6g; Fiber: 1g; Sugar: 3g; Protein: 6g; Sodium: 304mg

SIMPLE STEAMED SEITAN

NUT-FREE

Serves 4 / Prep time: 10 minutes / Cook time: 30 minutes

Seitan is surprisingly easy to make but can seem intimidating. Like, right now you may have freaked out just a little when you saw 13 ingredients. Don't worry! You're going to prep this in under 10 minutes, form cutlets, and steam. That's it! I suspect you might feel like a culinary rock star when you're done.

¾ cup vital wheat gluten

1 tablespoon rolled oats

1 tablespoon garbanzo bean flour

1 tablespoon nutritional yeast

¼ teaspoon garlic powder

¼ teaspoon black pepper

¼ teaspoon ground cumin

¼ teaspoon ground sage

¼ teaspoon smoked paprika

½ cup vegetable broth

1 tablespoon soy sauce

2 teaspoons olive oil

1 teaspoon blackstrap molasses

1. In a large bowl or stand mixer bowl, combine the vital wheat gluten, oats, garbanzo bean flour, nutritional yeast, garlic powder, pepper, cumin, sage, and paprika. Add the broth, soy sauce, oil, and molasses. Mix well and knead for 5 minutes by hand or by using the dough hook of the stand mixer, until it has a slightly tacky consistency, similar to bread dough.

2. Divide the dough into four equal parts (about 2½ ounces each). Place each on a parchment paper square, fold the parchment paper over, and press down to form the seitan into a square. Fold up in the parchment, then wrap each piece in aluminum foil.

3. In a large pot on the stove, pour 1 cup of water and insert a steamer basket. Place the wrapped seitan pieces in the basket. Bring the water to a boil. Cover and steam until the seitan is firm, about 30 minutes. You can use right away or store. See tip below.

Make It Ahead: This can be prepared up to 5 days in advance and refrigerated or frozen for up to 3 months.

Per serving: Calories: 151; Total fat: 3g; Total carbs: 10g; Fiber: 2g; Sugar: 1g; Protein: 21g; Sodium: 330mg

Measurement Conversions

OVEN TEMPERATURES

FAHRENHEIT	CELSIUS (APPROXIMATE)
250°F	120°C
300°F	150°C
325°F	165°C
350°F	180°C
375°F	190°C
400°F	200°C
425°F	220°C
450°F	230°C

VOLUME EQUIVALENTS (LIQUID)

US STANDARD	US STANDARD (OUNCES)	METRIC (APPROXIMATE)
2 tablespoons	1 fl. oz.	30 mL
¼ cup	2 fl. oz.	60 mL
½ cup	4 fl. oz.	120 mL
1 cup	8 fl. oz.	240 mL
1½ cups	12 fl. oz.	355 mL
2 cups or 1 pint	16 fl. oz.	475 mL
4 cups or 1 quart	32 fl. oz.	1 L
1 gallon	128 fl. oz.	4 L

WEIGHT EQUIVALENTS

US STANDARD	METRIC (APPROXIMATE)
½ ounce	15 g
1 ounce	30 g
2 ounces	60 g
4 ounces	115 g
8 ounces	225 g
12 ounces	340 g
16 ounces or 1 pound	455 g

VOLUME EQUIVALENTS (DRY)

US STANDARD	METRIC (APPROXIMATE)
⅛ teaspoon	0.5 mL
¼ teaspoon	1 mL
½ teaspoon	2 mL
¾ teaspoon	4 mL
1 teaspoon	5 mL
1 tablespoon	15 mL
¼ cup	59 mL
⅓ cup	79 mL
½ cup	118 mL
⅔ cup	156 mL
¾ cup	177 mL
1 cup	235 mL
2 cups or 1 pint	475 mL
3 cups	700 mL
4 cups or 1 quart	1 L

References

Barnard N. D., A. R. Scialli, P. Bertron, D. Hurlock, K. Edmonds, and L. Taley. "Effectiveness of a Low-Fat Vegetarian Diet in Altering Serum Lipids in Healthy Premenopausal Women." *American Journal of Cardiology* 85, no. 8 (April 15, 2000): 969–72.

Melina, Vesanto, Winston Craig, and Susan Levin. "Position of the Academy of Nutrition and Dietetics: Vegetarian Diets." *Journal of the Academy of Nutrition and Dietetics* 116, no. 12 (December 2016): 1970–80.

Messina, Virginia, and JL Fields. *Vegan for Her: The Woman's Guide to Being Healthy and Fit on a Plant-Based Diet*. Boston: Da Capo Lifelong Books, 2013.

Norris, Jack, and Virginia Messina. *Vegan for Life: Everything You Need to Know to Be Healthy and Fit on a Plant-Based Diet*. Boston: Da Capo Lifelong Books, 2011.

Sabate, J., K. Oda, and E. Ros. "Nut Consumption and Blood Lipid Levels: A Pooled Analysis of 25 Intervention Trials." *Archives of Internal Medicine* 170, no. 9 (May 10, 2010): 821–7.

THE DIRTY DOZEN AND THE CLEAN FIFTEEN™

A nonprofit environmental watchdog organization called Environmental Working Group (EWG) looks at data supplied by the US Department of Agriculture (USDA) and the Food and Drug Administration (FDA) about pesticide residues. Each year it compiles a list of the best and worst pesticide loads found in commercial crops. You can use these lists to decide which fruits and vegetables to buy organic to minimize your exposure to pesticides and which produce is considered safe enough to buy conventionally. This does not mean they are pesticide-free, though, so wash these fruits and vegetables thoroughly. The list is updated annually, and you can find it online at EWG.org/FoodNews.

DIRTY DOZEN™

1. strawberries
2. spinach
3. nectarines
4. apples
5. grapes
6. peaches
7. cherries
8. pears
9. tomatoes
10. celery
11. potatoes
12. sweet bell peppers

†Additionally, nearly three-quarters of hot pepper samples contained pesticide residues.

CLEAN FIFTEEN™

1. avocados
2. sweet corn*
3. pineapples
4. cabbages
5. onions
6. sweet peas (frozen)
7. papayas*
8. asparagus
9. mangoes
10. eggplants
11. honeydew melons
12. kiwis
13. cantaloupes
14. cauliflower
15. broccoli

* A small amount of sweet corn, papaya, and summer squash sold in the United States is produced from genetically modified seeds. Buy organic varieties of these crops if you want to avoid genetically modified produce.

Recipe Index by Dietary Label

RECIPE	GLUTEN-FREE	NUT-FREE	OIL-FREE	SOY-FREE
Açaí (or Not) Breakfast Bowl	x		x	x
Any Hummus Wrap	x	x	x	x
Artichoke Heart Salad	x	x	x	x
Avocado Black Bean Medley	x	x	x	x
Avocado Not-Toast	x	x	x	x
Avocado-Citrus Kale Salad	x	x	x	x
Awesome Overnight Oats	x	x	x	x
Bac'n Broccoli Rice Skillet	x	x	x	
Baked Butter Beans	x	x		x
Baked Ratatouille	x	x		x
Barbecue Tofu	x	x	x	
Basic Buddha Burrito Bowl	x	x	x	x
Black Bean and Sweet Potato Tacos	x	x	x	x
Breakfast Burrito	x	x	x	x
Burrito Lettuce Wraps	x	x	x	x
Cashew Dressing	x		x	x
Cashew Tempeh Stir-Fry	x			
Cauliflower Fried Rice	x	x	x	x
Chana Masala	x	x	x	x
Cheezy Zucchini Lasagna	x	x		
Chipotle Lentils	x	x	x	x
Ch-ofu Ricotta	x	x	x	
Coconut Curry Soup	x	x	x	x
Collard Green Bean Bake	x	x		x
Creamy Portobello Soup	x	x	x	x
Cucumber Zoodle Bowl	x	x	x	x
Delectable Dal	x	x	x	x
Easy as Shepherd's Pie	x	x	x	x
Easy Minestrone	x	x	x	x
Edamame Peanut Slaw	x		x	

RECIPE	GLUTEN-FREE	NUT-FREE	OIL-FREE	SOY-FREE
Edamame Sushi Rice	x	x	x	
Egg-y Salad	x	x		
Everyday Vegetable Broth	x	x	x	x
Falafel-style Burgers	x	x		x
Fast and Easy Fruit "Compote"	x	x	x	x
Fast Oats	x	x	x	x
Five Fruit Salad	x	x	x	x
Fruit and Veggie Gazpacho	x	x		x
Jacked-Up Hearts of Palm Fritters	x	x	x	x
Jackfruit Philly Cheesesteak Bowl	x	x	x	x
Kale Pesto Penne	x		x	x
Lentil Loaf Squares	x	x	x	
Lentil Veggie Flautas	x	x	x	x
Lucky Beans and Greens	x	x	x	x
Macro Miso Soup	x	x	x	
Marinara Sauce	x	x	x	x
Marinated Mushroom Sandwich	x	x		x
Mashed (Riced) Cauliflower	x	x	x	x
Mmm Mmm Umami Queso	x		x	
Mushroom Sloppy Joe Sandwich	x	x	x	x
Mushroom Stroganoff Bake	x	x		x
No-Chicken Pecan Salad	x	x		
Green Chile Black Bean Burgers	x	x	x	x
Oat Milk	x	x	x	x
One-Pot Hippie Bowl	x	x	x	x
One-Pot Mac	x	x	x	x
Paprika Potato Soup	x	x	x	
Peanut Sauce	x		x	
Peanutty Carrot Noodles	x		x	x
Perfect Pasta Under Pressure	x	x	x	x
Pita Pizza, Too	x	x	x	x
Potato and Pinto Bean Hash	x	x	x	x

RECIPE	GLUTEN-FREE	NUT-FREE	OIL-FREE	SOY-FREE
Protein Pasta Primavera	x	x	x	x
Quinoa Rainbow Chard	x	x	x	x
Red Jackfruit Jambalaya	x	x	x	x
Red "Risotto"	x	x	x	x
Roasted Japanese Yams and Tempeh	x	x	x	
Roasted Kabocha Squash with Chickpeas	x	x	x	x
Salad Pita Pizza	x	x	x	x
Savory Oats	x	x	x	x
Sheet Pan Lasagna	x	x	x	
Sheet Pan Pota-chos	x	x		x
Simple Vegan Sour Cream	x	x	x	
Simple Spicy Tostadas	x	x		x
Simple Steamed Seitan		x		
Skillet Seitan Stew	x	x	x	x
Smoky Coleslaw	x	x	x	x
Socca Bread Pizza	x	x		x
Spaghetti Squash Marinara	x	x	x	x
Spanish Quinoa Casserole	x	x	x	x
Speedy Corn Chowder	x	x	x	x
Spicy Pinto Bean Skillet	x	x	x	x
Spicy Quinoa Pilaf	x	x	x	x
Veggie Spring Rolls	x		x	x
Super Smoothie	x	x	x	x
Sweet Potato Alfredo	x			x
Tahini Roasted Vegetables	x	x		x
Tasty Tabouli		x	x	x
Texas Chili	x	x	x	x
Three-Bean Bonanza	x	x	x	x
Tofu Scalloped Potatoes	x	x		
Tofu-Spinach Casserole	x	x	x	
Tomato Tofu Scramble	x	x	x	
Two-Alarm Chili	x	x	x	x

RECIPE	GLUTEN-FREE	NUT-FREE	OIL-FREE	SOY-FREE
Tzatziki	x	x	x	
Umami Bean Dip	x	x	x	x
Vegan Corned Beef and Cabbage		x	x	x
Warm Cabbage Salad	x	x	x	x
Warm Fava Bean and Hearts of Palm Salad	x	x	x	x
White Bean Pesto Salad	x		x	

Recipe Index by Meal Type

Index

Acknowledgments

Callisto Media, I love you! I love working with every single team member to create meaningful content that helps people make healthy and delicious food, which in turn helps the planet and the animals. Many thanks to my editors Pam Kingsley for her careful and patient guidance (and for being so open to this vegan's desire to speak the plant-based language that has redefined the food movement) and Pamela Ellgen for understanding my desire to keep this book friendly to the home cook.

A shout-out to the Colorado Springs Vegan Cooking Academy students: Thank for letting me test recipes on you!

A lifelong thanks to Janice and Larry Fields, my parents, who have always supported me — and to my sisters Dana and Dee Ann and my niece Paige and nephew Ethan for doing the same. Special thanks to my Aunt Candy, who is the unofficial president of my nonexistent fan club.

The biggest thanks of all must go to Dave Burgess, my husband and best friend. His support is why I get to follow my vegan passion—in work and play—every day. He's also a great human parent to our furry babes, Oliver and Harry.

ABOUT THE AUTHOR

JL FIELDS is a vegan chef, coach, and consultant. She is the founder and culinary director of the Colorado Springs Vegan Cooking Academy and a Master Vegan Lifestyle Coach and Educator. JL is the author of several cookbooks, including *Vegan Meal Prep: Ready-To-Go Meals and Snacks for Healthy Plant-Based Eating*; *Vegan Pressure Cooking: Delicious Beans, Grains and One-Pot Meals in Minutes*; and *The Vegan Air Fryer: The Healthier Way to Enjoy Deep-Fried Flavors*. She writes the monthly vegan dining review for the Colorado Springs *Gazette* and lives in Colorado Springs with her husband Dave, cat Oliver, and dog Harry.

Website: JLGoesVegan.com

Facebook: Facebook.com/JLGoesVegan

Instagram: @JLGoesVegan